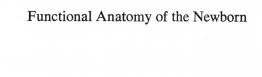

Functional Anatomy of the Newborn

Functional Anatomy

of the Newborn

Edmund S. Crelin, Ph.D., D.Sc.

Professor of Anatomy

Yale University School of Medicine

New Haven and London, Yale University Press, 1973

Library of Congress catalog card number: 72–91292
International standard book number: 0–300–01632–8 (cloth)
0–300–01633–6 (paper)

Designed by John O. C. McCrillis
and set in Times Roman type.
Printed in the United States of America by
Connecticut Printers, Incorporated
Hartford, Connecticut.

Published in Great Britain, Europe, and Africa by
Yale University Press, Ltd., London.
Distributed in Canada by McGill-Queen's University
Press, Montreal; in Latin America by Kaiman & Polon,
Inc., New York City; in Australasia and Southeast
Asia by John Wiley & Sons Australasia Pty. Ltd.,
Sydney; in India by UBS Publishers' Distributors Pvt.,
Ltd., Delhi; in Japan by John Weatherhill, Inc., Tokyo.

For the 2,020 Yale Medical Students
I Have Had the Privilege to Teach

Contents

Illustrations following page 71

Preface

As a consultant to the Newborn Special Care Unit of the Yale–New Haven Medical Center I assist in the evaluation of newborn infants with birth defects. In the beginning I found it difficult to do because I could not find a single publication containing the functional anatomical information I needed on the newborn infant. As I began to compile this information from a multitude of sources, including my own studies, I put it into mimeographed form for my colleagues. Those who were able to use it to great advantage were the obstetricians and the pediatric internists, surgeons, radiologists, pathologists, and nurses. From this experience I decided to write a concise guide to be used by all personnel involved in one form or another with the newborn infant, including students.

The newborn infant is *not* a miniature adult. In this book, therefore, those parts of functional anatomy that differ from the adult to the greatest degree receive the greatest emphasis. Since the newborn infant is still in the process of developing into a mature individual, I include the times during prenatal development when structures first appear and/or function, as well as the times after birth that other structures first appear and/or function. To add to the usefulness of the book by paramedical personnel such information as pulse rate, blood pressure, body temperature, breathing rate, blood cell counts, etc. is included.

I drew three illustrations I felt would have the most general clinical relevance. The information for these was gathered directly from observations I made on living newborn infants and from dissections I performed on newborn cadavers. The readers who desire a more graphic knowledge of newborn infant anatomy are referred to the first and, at present, the only complete and detailed published book on the subject: *Anatomy of the Newborn: An Atlas* (E. S. Crelin; Philadelphia, Lea and Febiger, 1969). Many of its color illustrations are life size. As an aid to interested readers of the present synopsis, the sequence of body parts of this book are arranged in the same order that they appear in the *Atlas*.

There is still much to be learned about the human newborn infant, especially its physiology. Some recently derived data from investigations on fetal and newborn animals are included when there is every indication that the conditions are almost exactly the same in the human fetus and newborn infant.

I wish to thank my friend and colleague, Alexander Campbell, M.D., associate professor of pediatrics and director of the Newborn Special Care Unit of the Yale–New Haven Medical Center, for critically reading most of the manuscript of this book.

E. S. Crelin

New Haven, Connecticut
1972

Body Weight, Size, and Proportions

The average full-term newborn infant (8½ months) weighs about 3,300 gm (7 lb). The average crown–heel length (top of the head to the sole of the foot) is about 50 cm (20 inches). On the average the newborn male is slightly larger and heavier than the newborn female. Body length and weight are usually proportionate. A premature newborn infant (7 months) weighing only 1,200 gm (3 lb) would have a crown–heel length of about 38 cm (16 inches). The absolute increase in the weight of the body after birth is about twenty times. Water constitutes 80 percent of the total body weight at birth, whereas it constitutes 60 percent in adulthood. At birth 45 percent of the water is extracellular and 35 percent is intracellular; in adulthood 17 percent is extracellular and 43 percent intracellular. Organ size and weight are usually proportionate to the total body weight. No matter what the overall body size and weight are at birth, the relative proportions of the head, trunk, and limbs are about the same (Fig. A). The crown–heel length is equal to about four times the size of the head; it is about eight times in the adult. The pelvis and lower limbs are relatively much smaller than they are in the adult. The lower limbs, besides being underdeveloped at birth in relationship to the upper limbs, are bowed and kept folded in the same position as before birth. The umbilicus is located about 1.5 cm below the midpoint between the crown and the heel. As the pelvis and lower limbs grow, the umbilicus assumes a higher position. At one year after birth it is midway between the crown and heel, and in the adult three-fifths of the body length is caudal to the umbilicus.

Hair and Sebaceous Glands

About the fourth month of development, fetal hair begins to grow, first on the head and then on the rest of the body. This first crop of hairs is the lanugo and is well developed by the seventh fetal month. Some of these delicate primary hairs, of varying pigmentation, are shed before birth and the remainder shortly after birth. The last to be shed are those of the eyelashes, eyebrows, and scalp. The fine lanugo hairs are replaced by secondary hairs that are also fine (down). At about the time of puberty, coarser, longer, and more deeply pigmented terminal hairs begin to develop in specific regions of the body according to the sex of the individual.

Sebaceous glands arise from the sides of the developing hair follicles of the fetus during the fourth month of development. The secretion of the glands is responsible for the natural oiliness of the hair and skin in the adult. In the fetus the oily secretion gathers as a layer coating the skin to protect it against the constant exposure to amniotic fluid. The sebaceous secretion is the chief constituent of the whitish cheesy material, the vernix caseosa, coating the skin surface of the full-term infant at birth. It accumulates in noticeable quantities where the lanugo hairs are thickest, i.e. the eyelashes, eyebrows, and scalp. The external acoustic meatus is filled with vernix caseosa at birth.

Adipose Tissue

Most of the subcutaneous adipose tissue develops during the last weeks of pregnancy. This causes the full-term infant to appear much more robust than a premature one; the neck and limbs of the premature infant, especially the lower limbs, are noticeably thinner. Since the newborn infant has a larger surface-to-body-weight ratio than the adult, the infant has a greater physical problem in maintaining body temperature. Some of the adipose tissue developed during the last few weeks of a full-term pregnancy is brown fat. It is related to the mammalian hibernating gland and is important in body-temperature regulation and as a site of heat production. This brown fat forms a subcutaneous sheet around the neck and between the scapulas that causes the neck of a full-term infant to appear short and thick (Figs. A, B, C). Brown fat is also located as a thin sheet deep to the sternum and as thick masses immediately behind the suprarenal glands and kidneys (the pararenal fat pads). Even though the premature infant may lack brown fat it does possess adipose tissues that serves an important functional space-filling role, such as the fat body of the ischiorectal fossa, the orbital fat body, and the buccal fat pad. After birth these space-filling fat masses are only slightly diminished in extreme cases of emaciation. Fibrous fat pads are present in the newborn infant that serve as future cushions in the palms and fingers and especially in the soles and toes. The plantar fat pads make the newborn infant appear to have flat feet.

Fat depots that ordinarily serve as stored metabolic fuel after birth are generally lacking or present in only small amounts in the full-term infant. They are described in relationship to specific organs. The general lack of adipose tissue is not nutritionally detrimental because before birth the principal metabolic fuel (calories) of the fetus is carbohydrate that is continuously supplied by the mother through the placenta. Near term there is an accumulation of large reserves of carbohydrate in the liver and skeletal muscle that help tide the infant over the transitional period between birth and the time when suckling is established at about three days after birth. From then on the infant's principal fuel is fat.

The temperature of the full-term infant at birth is the same or slightly higher than that of its mother, or about 98.8° F. There is an immediate 3.0° F fall in the temperature of the infant after birth even when an attempt is made to prevent it. The rectal temperature one hour after birth is about 95.8° F (36.7° C). However, during the first two hours after birth there may be a fall as great as 5.0° F without any marked disturbance of the environmental temperature.

Mammary Glands

The mammary glands at birth are firm, flat, round masses of tissue about 1 cm in diameter and 7 mm thick, and each weighs about 1 gm (Fig. B). There is a depression in the center of the areola containing the nipple. A few days after birth the glands in both sexes usually become swollen and elevated 2 cm or more above the chest surface. A few drops of opalescent gray fluid known as colostrum (witch's milk) may exude from the nipple. This is the result of the stimulating effect of the maternal hormones that crossed the placenta before birth.

With the growth of the thorax the areolas gradually move farther apart. This results in the mammary line of the adult being both relatively and absolutely farther from the median plane of the body than it is in the newborn infant.

Skeleton

The process of ossification of the skeleton begins as discrete foci known as centers of ossification in either membrane or cartilage. In man, most of them appear in cartilage. The first center appears in the shaft of the clavicle at six weeks of development. Of over 800 ossification centers that form in the human body, slightly more than half appear after birth. Nearly all the bones of the adult are formed from two or more centers. There are primary and secondary ossification centers; the primary form the greater part of a bone and almost all of them appear before birth (Fig. A). Except for the condylar centers of the femur and tibia and possibly the center of the head of the humerus, secondary ossification centers are formed after birth. The postnatal centers appear sooner in females than in males. Their appearance is measured first by days, then months, then years. Likewise, the completion of ossification of the skeleton occurs earlier in females, by as much as one to two years in the late teens.

The bones of the newborn infant are much more spongy or porous in structure than those of the adult. This is due in part to the lack of functional stress that the bones are subjected to before birth. The fetus is in an essentially weightless state surrounded by amniotic fluid. Even so there is sufficient mineral present to allow the ossified parts of the skeleton of a newborn infant to be seen on an X-ray film (Fig. A). With the exception of the vertebral column all the other parts of the skeleton undergo a reduction in porosity after birth. This is related to a reduction in the hematopoietic regions where new blood cells form in the marrow of the skeleton. At birth, hematopoiesis occurs in the red marrow of all the bones of the skeleton as the primary source of nearly every type of blood cell. In the adult, hematopoiesis is limited to the red marrow of cancellous bone, chiefly in the bodies of the vertebrae, the ribs, sternum, diploe of the skull, and proximal ends of the humerus and femur.

The number of bones in the average full-term infant is 270 (172 in the axial skeleton and 98 in the appendicular skeleton). Except for the small sesamoid bones, there are 206 bones in the adult (80 in the axial skeleton and 126 in the appendicular skeleton). This difference in the number of bones is due to the fusion of what were separate bones at birth and the formation of additional ones after birth. The skeleton, including both the bones and cartilage, constitutes from 15 to 20 percent of the total weight of the newborn infant. The increase in the weight of the skeleton from birth to adulthood is about twenty times. More detailed descriptions of parts of the skeleton are in the sections describing specific regions of the body.

Musculature and Connective Tissues

The muscles of the body of the newborn infant constitute about 25 percent of the entire body weight, whereas in the adult they constitute about 40 to 45 percent. In the newborn infant the muscles of the head and trunk constitute a little over 40 percent of the total weight of the musculature; in the adult this figure is reduced to from 25 to 30 percent because of the relative increase in the amount of limb musculature. The upper limb musculature, relatively well developed in the newborn infant, constitutes only 18 to 20 percent of the total muscle weight in the adult. In contrast, the lower limb musculature, relatively underdeveloped in the newborn infant, constitutes as much as 55 percent of the total muscle weight in the adult.

All of the skeletal and cardiac muscle fibers an individual will ever have are formed before birth. Skeletal muscle fibers are all present by the fourth month of development and all the cardiac muscle fibers by the eighth or ninth month. Therefore the growth of muscles after birth is by an increase in the volume of the individual fibers and not by an increase in their number.

The size of muscle fibers is related to their activity. As soon as the fibers differentiate from mesenchyme in the embryo, they undergo contractions. Individual skeletal muscles begin to contract during the seventh week of development when the cartilaginous skeleton is complete. However, not until the fourth month of development does the mother first become aware of fetal movements known as the "quickening."

Between the third and fourth weeks of development the first heartbeats occur, while the heart is still a single tube. From then on the heart muscle must continuously contract intermittently throughout the life of the individual. The heart musculature of the newborn infant is therefore well developed, as are other muscles that undergo a fair amount of activity before birth; they are usually associated with functions essential to the newborn infant for independent existence. The diaphragm and trunk muscles associated with expansion and contraction of the thoracic cavity contract spasmodically (hiccoughs) before birth. This exercises the muscles that are needed for breathing immediately after birth. The first breath of life requires very high intrathoracic pressures produced by muscle contraction to expand the lungs with air.

The muscles of facial expression are relatively well developed at the time of birth. The orbicularis oculi muscles can contract firmly to protect the eyes. The muscles of the lips, jaws, tongue, palate, and pharynx are well developed in the newborn infant for suckling and swallowing. The first circumscribed neuromuscular reflexes that appear before birth are those associated with suckling and swallowing. Specific localized reflexes, such as opening the mouth, occur as early as eleven weeks of development when the oral region, supplied by the maxillary and mandibular divisions of the trigeminal nerve, is stimulated. The fetus begins to swallow amniotic fluid as early as twelve and a half weeks of development. Near term it swallows as much as 750 ml a day. Afferent nerves involved in the suckling and swallowing reflexes are the sensory branches (infraorbital, mental, buccal, lingual, palatine) of the trigeminal nerve (5th cranial) distributed about the lips, oral cavity and tongue, and the glossopharyngeal nerve (9th cranial) branches to the tongue and pharynx. Efferent nerves involved in these reflexes are the motor branches of the facial nerve (7th cranial) to the muscles of facial expression, including the buccinator muscle, the trigeminal nerve branches to the muscles of mastication, the hypoglossal nerve (12th cranial) branches to the muscles of the tongue, and the vagus nerve (10th cranial) branches to the muscles of the pharynx.

The upper limbs have a fair range of motion before birth. When the fingers of the fetus brush against its lips it can grasp one with its mouth and suckle it just as the infant suckles its mother's nipple after birth. The grasp of the hand at birth is quite strong; however, it is not so strong or sustained as that of a newborn monkey or ape that can cling firmly to a very active tree-swinging mother.

The normal cramped position of the lower limbs in the uterus does not allow for much movement. Before birth the joints and their related muscles depend upon muscle activity to produce a minimal range of movement for normal development. Therefore it is not uncommon to find ankle-joint abnormalities in a newborn infant where the range of joint motion in the uterus was greatly restricted. The fetus is essentially in a weightless state in the amniotic fluid; therefore the neck and trunk musculature do not develop sufficiently to support the relatively large, heavy head for some time after birth.

In general the skeletal muscles of a newborn infant contain relatively more muscle tissue and less collagenous connective tissue than those of an adult. Also, the connective tissues of the entire body, including the fascias and aponeuroses, are more delicate at birth than in later life. Some sheets of muscle and their connective tissue sheaths, such as the levator ani muscle, are so flimsy at birth that they have the consistency of moist tissue paper. Exceptions are the firm, collagenous tendons at the wrist, fingers, ankles, and toes. The synovial sheaths of these tendons are fully developed at birth. Likewise, the submuscular and subfascial bursae throughout the body are fully developed at birth, except the subcutaneous bursae which may or may not be.

Lymph Nodes and Thoracic Duct

At birth the size of both individual and groups of lymph nodes varies from microscopic proportions to masses covering an area 1×1 cm. The largest single mass is usually made up of the superficial inguinal lymph nodes. A large group of subgroups is in the axilla. Nodes that are just visible to the naked eye are found in the head and neck, upper limb, thorax, abdomen, pelvis, and lower limb. The natural color of the nodes is pink.

The total amount of lymphoid tissue segregated into lymph nodes in the newborn infant is considerable. There is an increase in the amount during childhood that is largely due to the growth of nodes already present at birth, rather than the formation of new nodes. For example, the average weight of individual mesenteric lymph nodes increases nearly twenty times between birth and adulthood, whereas the total number of these nodes increases only about three times. The lymphatic tissues found in specific organs, including the tonsils and thymus, are described with the body regions in which they are located.

The formation of lymphocytes (lymphopoiesis) occurs in the liver, the marrow of the skeleton, and possibly the thymus at two and a half months of fetal development. They cease to be formed in the liver before birth. At four months of development lymphocytes begin to be produced in the lymph nodes. The lymphopoietic activity of the spleen becomes evident at birth.

The thoracic duct in both the newborn infant and adult is the largest single lymph vessel in the body. It begins deep to the right crus of the diaphragm. A dilatation at its origin, the cisterna chyli, may or may not be present. From its origin to where it opens into the junction of the left internal jugular and left subclavian veins, it is about 10 to 11 cm in length. The right lymphatic duct that drains lymph from the right side of the head and neck and from the right upper limb is difficult to visualize, because it may be only 2 or 3 mm long and surrounded by lymph nodes or it may consist of three tiny vessels instead of one.

Vertebral Column

The average length of the free vertebral column (from the first cervical to the fifth lumbar vertebra) is 19 or 20 cm at birth. It is equal to about 40 percent of the total body length (Figs. A, C). In the newborn infant the cervical part constitutes about a fourth, the thoracic part a half, and the lumbar part a fourth of the entire free column. In the adult the thoracic portion also constitutes about half of the total free column, but the lumbar part is increased to nearly a third while the cervical part is reduced to a fifth, or a sixth of the entire column.

The free vertebral column has no fixed curves at birth. It is so flexible that the column dissected free from the body can easily be bent (flexed or extended) into a perfect half circle. After birth the thoracic part gradually develops a relatively fixed curve. A flexible cervical curve appears when the infant is able to lift its head, and a flexible lumbar curve appears at the end of the first or beginning of the second year when the child starts to walk.

At birth each vertebra of the free column, except the first and second cervicals, consists of three separate ossification centers joined by hyaline cartilage (Fig. A). The first cervical vertebra (atlas) consists of only two bony centers, whereas the second cervical (axis) consists of four ossification centers—one for the body, two for the neural arches, and one for the dens. The four centers fuse into a single bone between the third and sixth years after birth. The atlas becomes a completely bony ring between the fifth and ninth years. The bodies of all the vertebrae of the free column, except the axis, more than double their transverse and sagittal diameters between birth and adulthood. At birth the future gelatinous shock absorber of the vertebral column, the nucleus pulposus, constitutes the greater part of the intervertebral discs (Fig. C). In the adult, fibrous cartilage (anulus fibrosus) constitutes the greater part of the discs. The sacral and coccygeal parts of the vertebral column are described with the bony pelvis.

External Male Genitals

The penis and especially the scrotum are relatively large in the newborn infant. The body of the penis is usually slender and the glans is usually more tapered at the tip than that of the adult. Its length is about 2.5 cm and its maximum width is 1.0 cm. Although the separation of the fused prepuce and glans begins as early as the fifth month of development they may be incompletely separated at birth. Even though the erectile tissue contains less smooth muscle and elastic tissue than it does in the adult, the penis is capable of a firm erection. The total length of the urethra at birth is about 6.2 cm long. The spongiosal part is about 4.6 cm, the membranous part 0.8 cm, and the prostatic part 0.8 cm. The urethra almost triples its length between birth and adulthood, with most of the growth occurring in the spongiosal part.

The scrotum in the newborn infant has a broad base that does not begin to become narrower than the rest of the sac until a year or more after birth. The width at its base is 2.0 cm and the length of the relaxed scrotum about 3.0 cm. Both the walls and the septum of the scrotum at birth are relatively much thicker than in adulthood.

At birth both testes weigh about 0.85 gm and both epididymides weigh about 0.24 gm. The relative weight of the testes is about the same in the newborn infant and the adult. They weigh about 40 to 50 gm in the adult. The testis at birth averages about 10 mm in length and 5 mm in thickness (Fig. B). It increases four times in length and a little more than four times in thickness between birth and adulthood. The long axis of the testis is almost vertical in the newborn infant (Fig. B). Androgen is produced in the testes as early as the ninth week of development; it plays an important role in the differentiation of the male genitals and secondary sexual characteristics in the fetus. The testes lack spermatozoa at birth because the spermatozoa do not begin to differentiate until late in puberty.

The spermatic cord is relatively thicker in the newborn infant than in the adult. It passes almost vertically through the inguinal rings and canal to the scrotum (Fig. B). The superficial inguinal ring at birth is not so displaced medially from the deep inguinal ring as it is in adulthood. The inguinal canal of the newborn infant is therefore relatively shorter as well as more vertical than that of the adult. The cremaster muscle of the spermatic cord is well developed at birth.

The testes are at the site of the future deep inguinal rings from the sixth to the seventh month of fetal life. Prior to the migration of the testis into the scrotum (descent), the relatively compact undifferentiated mesenchymal wall, where the inguinal rings will form, swells into a large gelatinous mass, the gubernaculum testis. The swelling is due to an increase in the mesenchymal ground substance, which has a high content of acid mucopolysaccharide composed largely of hyaluronic acid. This jelly-like material is similar in structure and composition to the gelatinous ground substance of the umbilical cord (Wharton's jelly) and the vitreous body of the eyeball. The gubernaculum is directly connected to the testis and epididymis and the adjacent peritoneum that forms the processus vaginalis. It is not directly continuous with the skin and dartos tunic of the future scrotum because a separation zone or fascial cleft separates the two. As this gelatinous mass enlarges, it bulges anteriorly and expands the walls of the scrotum. At the same time a tubular extension of the peritoneum, the processus vaginalis, invades the mass. Under hormonal influence between the seventh and eighth months of development, the gubernaculum undergoes marked shrinkage while the testis, which is attached to the processus vaginalis, passes into the scrotum along with it. The left testis usually migrates into the scrotum a little ahead of the right. The part of the shrunken mesenchyme that forms a tubular prolongation of the anterior abdominal wall investing the testis, epididymis, processus vaginalis, ductus deferens, and testicular vessels differentiates into the three layers of the spermatic cord: the external spermatic, cremasteric, and internal spermatic fascias. The fascias of the three muscle layers of the rest of the anterior abdominal wall differentiate before those of the extension of the wall that later form the inguinal rings and the coverings of the spermatic cord. When the three fascial layers of the cord do differentiate they establish a direct continuity with the fascial layers of the abdominal wall—the external spermatic fascia with the fascia (intercrural fibers) of the external abdominal oblique muscle; the cremasteric fascia with the fascia of the internal oblique muscle and its extension, the cremasteric muscle; the internal spermatic fascia with the fascia of the transversus abdominis muscle (transversalis fascia).

The distal end of the gelatinous extension of the abdominal wall is the last to completely shrink and differentiate into ordinary fibrous connective tissue. This occurs after birth. Therefore, what appears to be a large tail of the epididymis in the newborn male is actually mesenchymal remains of the gubernaculum testis surrounding a relatively very small tail of the epididymis. Since the gubernaculum testis was never attached to the wall of the scrotum, the testis and its epididymis and surrounding fascial sheaths are separated from the dartos tunic of the scrotal wall of the newborn male by a fascial cleft.

In 90 percent of full-term newborn infants the testes have completed their migration into the scrotum. However, in a premature infant the migration may be incomplete, with the scrotum distended more with gelatinous gubernacular tissue than with testes.

The tubular projection of peritoneum, the processus vaginalis, that passed into the scrotum with the testis, almost completely envelops the testis as a double-walled, friction-reducing sac, the tunica vaginalis. The tunica may contain a relatively large amount of fluid that is absorbed shortly after birth. The lumen of the portion of the processus vaginalis between the tunica and the deep inguinal ring is collapsed at birth but not necessarily obliterated. It is patent in 66 percent of male infants up to two weeks of age. In 80 percent of male infants between ten and twenty days of age the processus is partially if not completely obliterated. The left processus usually becomes obliterated before the right. Even when it is obliterated at birth, a small peritoneal evagination is present at the deep inguinal ring. The danger of having a persistent patent processus is that abdominal contents can pass into it and result in an indirect congenital inguinal hernia.

External Female Genitals

The labia majora are relatively large at birth and are united by a definite posterior labial commissure. In the full-term female an encapsulated tube of fat that is deep to a thin layer of subcutaneous fat extends from the inguinal region on each side into the labium majus. Buried in the upper end of each tube of fat is the flattened fibrous distal end of the round (teres) ligament of the uterus that can be traced through the superficial inguinal ring into the inguinal canal. Before birth the abdominal wall in the region of the future inguinal rings is undifferentiated mesenchyme that swells into a gelatinous mass of connective tissue ground substance consisting chiefly of acid mucopolysaccharide. This mass is continuous with a narrow tube of similar gelatinous mesenchyme that extends retroperitoneally to the ovary. The gelatinous mesenchyme is the homologue of the gubernaculum testis in the male. The swollen part of the future inguinal ring portion of the abdominal wall does not distend the labium majus to the degree that it does the scrotum in the male. At this time a short tube of peritoneum, the processus vaginalis, invades the gelatinous tissue of the undifferentiated abdominal wall. When the gelatinous material shrinks, the most distal part transforms into fibrous tissue that may be in the form of short bands that are equivalent to the fascial sheaths of the spermatic cord in the male, and a more proximal part becomes a short inguinal canal containing a nipple-like protrusion of peritoneum, the processus vaginalis. Gubernacular-type tissue from the inguinal canal to the ovary becomes a relatively long, round, collagenous ligament. The portion of this ligament from the deep inguinal ring to the uterus is known as the round ligament of the uterus; it is about 1.5 cm long. After it turns from the uterus to pass to the ovary it is known as the ovarian ligament, which is about 5.0 mm long. The lumen of the processus vaginalis does not become obliterated until after birth, when the left one is usually obliterated before the right one. The processus is still patent in 20 percent of female infants a year old. Even when it is obliterated at birth there is a small peritoneal evagination at the deep inguinal ring. The danger of having a patent processus vaginalis (canal of Nuck) is that abdominal contents can pass into it and result in an indirect congenital inguinal hernia.

The labia minora are relatively large flaps at birth. Each labium is about 2.5 mm thick, the length of the base of each is 2.0 cm and the widest part of the flap is 1.2 cm. The clitoris is relatively larger in the newborn female than in the adult (Fig. C). The length of the glans and body is around 1.0 cm. The hymen at birth is a thick elliptical ring of connective tissue surrounding the superficially positioned orifice of the vagina, which is normally patent (Figs. B, C). The mucosal membrane lining the hymen is smooth and thin. The orifice of the vagina in the newborn female will easily admit the little finger of an adult hand, with a circumference of about 5.0 cm. During early childhood the orifice becomes more deeply positioned and the mucosal lining of the hymen becomes a membranous fold along the posterior margin of the lumen of the vagina that narrows the lumen considerably. An imperforate or perforated hymeneal membrane forming a diaphragm completely across the vaginal lumen is a malformation.

Spinal Medulla (Cord) and Nerves

At birth the weight of the spinal medulla, excluding its dural covering and the spinal nerve roots, is 3 to 3.5 gm. This is about 12.5 percent of the adult weight. The spinal medulla constitutes about 1.0 percent of the body weight at birth, whereas it constitutes only about 0.25 percent in the adult. In the newborn the ratio of the spinal medulla weight to the weight of the brain is 1:110; in the adult it is 1:50. At birth the spinal medulla is 15 to 17 cm long or only a little more than a third as long as it is in the adult. The medulla at birth usually terminates at the lower level of the second or the upper level of the third lumbar vertebra (Fig. C).

Nerve cells that are ultimately capable of a rapid transmission of impulses become fully functional at about the time they are completely myelinated.

The formation of myelin in the spinal medulla begins during the middle of fetal life and is not completed in some fibers until after puberty. Myelin appears first in the cervical part of the medulla and then extends progressively to lower levels. The ventral motor root fibers acquire myelin before those of the dorsal sensory root. The last fibers to become myelinated are those of descending motor tracts, such as the corticospinal (pyramidal) and the tectospinal tracts, which are myelinated during the first and second years after birth.

The major trunks of the spinal nerves, especially those that form the brachial and sacral plexuses, are relatively much larger in the newborn infant than in the adult. The sciatic nerve in the infant is the largest single nerve trunk in the body, just as it is the adult. The intervertebral foramina of the newborn vertebral column, which transmit the spinal nerves, are also large, especially the lumbar foramina. However, the more terminal spinal nerve branches at birth are nearly microscopic in size.

The autonomic nerves in the newborn infant have the same general structure and relationships, especially the variations, as those in the adult. At birth the parasympathetic ganglia such as the ciliary, submandibular, pterygopalatine, and the otic are relatively small. As in the adult, the largest sympathetic ganglia in the body at birth are the superior cervicals, the cervicothoracics, and the celiacs. The plexuses of the autonomic nerves at birth, including those with mixtures of other types of neurons, such as the pharyngeal, cardiac, esophageal, celiac (pancreatic, splenic, phrenic), hepatic, gastric, mesenteric, renal, and aortic, and the hypogastrics (deferential, vesical, prostatic), resemble spider webs in size and structure. The great number of variations of the sympathetic nerves and ganglia are the same in the newborn infant as in the adult. For example, there is no constant pattern of the sympathetic trunk—the number and size of its ganglia and the number and size of its branches—on each side of the body. What is depicted in illustrations as the middle cervical ganglion in the newborn infant and adult is extremely variable. The variations in the origin, number, and size of the cervical and thoracic cardiac nerves are also great. The cardiac plexus is actually a single plexus that is artificially divided into superficial and deep parts.

Skull

The greater part of the head of the newborn infant surrounds the relatively massive brain; only a small part constitutes the face (Figs. A, B). These features of the head are reflected in the proportions: the preponderance of the calvarial portion of the newborn skull over the facial portion is striking. The distance from the top of the skull to the upper margin of the orbit is about 5.0 cm. The distance from the upper margin of the orbit to the bottom of the mandible is about 4.0 cm. The ratio between the calvarial and facial portions at birth is 8:1, whereas in the adult female the ratio is 2.5:1 and in the adult male 2:1. The thickness of the calvarial bones varies between 1.0 and 2.0 mm at birth. The calvarial part is also much larger in proportion to the base of the skull than it is in the adult. The width of the newborn face (8.0 cm) is relatively less in proportion to the calvarial part of the head than it is in the adult, but it is twice as broad in comparison to its height than in the adult. The orbits are large, broad, and rounded, with sharp margins (Fig. B). The anterior nasal aperture is large, broad, and round with a distinct anterior nasal spine. Its height is 1.4 cm and its greatest width is 1.1 cm. The upper and lower jaws are broad and very low at birth (Figs. A, B). Each jaw has a series of rounded elevations that contain the deciduous teeth.

The base of the newborn skull is small compared to the calvarial part that extends beyond it laterally and posteriorly. The hard palate is short and broad and the choanae are almost circular. The hard palate is 2.3 cm long and its greatest width is 2.2 cm. The posterior border of the vomer bone of the nasal septum at the choanae is relatively lower (6.5 mm in height) and more slanted than in the adult. The relatively short medial and lateral laminae of the pterygoid processes (1.4 cm in length) extend forward and outward at more of an acute angle with the base of the sphenoid bone than they do in the adult. With the absence of bony external acoustic meatuses, the tympanic rings that serve as attachments of the eardrums are prominent features of the base of the newborn skull. The occipital condyles are elongated and quite flat instead of curved as they are in the adult.

The skull as a whole grows relatively less after birth than the other major divisions of the skeleton. Between birth and adulthood the calvarial part increases four to five times and the facial part about twelve times in volume. During this same time the capacity of the calvarial part increases about three and a half times, or from about 400 cc to 1,300 or 1,500 cc. The horizontal circumference of the skull increases about 50 percent (from 33 cm to about 50 or 55 cm). Most of the postnatal skull growth occurs during the first two years. By two years of age the cranial capacity is about 950 cc and the horizontal circumference of the skull is about 47 cm. During this time the facial part of the skeleton grows more than the calvarial part, to some extent because of the increase in the size of the orbits which complete half their postnatal growth during the first two years after birth. Most of the postnatal growth of the lower portion of the facial part of the skull is due to the lateral expansion of the hard palate and the development of the maxillary sinuses.

Fonticuli (Fontanelles)

The bones of the calvarial portion of the newborn skull are quite thin and separated by flexible tough membrane along the suture lines of the skull. Expansions along the sutures are the fonticuli (Fig. A), six of which are normally present at birth. Two are median (anterior and posterior) and four are lateral (two sphenoid, two mastoid). Numerous small accessory fonticuli may be present at birth. The largest is the diamond-shaped anterior fonticulus that overlies the superior sagittal dural venous sinus (Figs. A, B, C). Thus the skin overlying the fonticulus pulsates. It has an average diameter of approximately 25 mm (1 inch) at birth. The anterior fonticulus undergoes a regular course of involution beginning about three months after birth. As with all the other fonticuli the obliteration is due to the progressive ingrowth of the edges of the membranous bones that form their borders. In over 90 percent of normal children the anterior is obliterated by two years of age. The mastoid fonticulus is also obliterated by the second year; however, the sphenoid is obliterated as early as six months after birth.

Frontal Bones

The frontal bones are separated by the median frontal (metopic) suture at birth. The suture is rarely present in the adult because it is usually obliterated between six and eight years of age. The frontal bones lack frontal sinuses at birth. The sinuses do not begin to invade the bones until about the second year after birth. The superciliary arches are also absent at birth (Fig. A). They appear in relationship to the development of the frontal sinuses, especially in the male after puberty. At birth the greatest length of each bone from the orbit to the coronal suture is 5.7 to 6.0 cm and the greatest width at the forehead is 5.0 to 5.5 cm. Its thickness is about 1.0 to 2.0 mm.

Sphenoid Bone

The sphenoid bone at birth consists of three separate parts: the body, the lesser wings, and the greater wings and pterygoid processes (Fig. C). The body of the sphenoid is composed of spongy bone at birth. The sphenoid sinuses do not begin to invade the bone until the fifth year of age. The three separate parts of the sphenoid unite during the first year after birth. The optic canal of the newborn infant is relatively large and may have the fetal shape of a keyhole or an inverted figure 8 instead of being circular as it usually is in the adult. The vertical diameter is about 4.0 mm and the transverse diameter 3.0 mm. A relatively large mass of cartilage separates the body of the sphenoid at birth from the basilar part of the occipital bone at the spheno-occipital synchondrosis (Figs. A, C). The vomer bone is a great distance (1.0 cm) from the synchondrosis at birth, whereas in the adult it overlaps the former site of the synchondrosis. Bony union of the sphenoid and occipital bones across the synchondrosis does not begin until shortly after puberty.

Occipital Bone

The occipital bone at birth consists of four separate parts: a basilar part, two lateral parts, and a squamous part (Fig. A). They are united by cartilage and arranged in a ring around the foramen magnum. The cartilage between the squamous and lateral parts is flexible at birth (obstetric joint). These parts usually begin to fuse together during the second year. The lateral parts generally unite with the basilar part during the third or fourth year after birth. However, the bony union of all of these parts may be delayed until seven years of age or later. The basilar part of the occipital bone at birth is not inclined toward the vertical plane as it is in later life. The bony roof of the nasopharynx therefore forms a shallow curve at birth instead of an abrupt deep arch. The length of the roof of the nasopharynx at birth is also relatively much longer than it is in the adult (Fig. C).

The foramen magnum is usually trapezium-shaped with an anteroposterior diameter of about 2.0 cm and an anteriorly located widest transverse diameter of 1.5 cm.

Ethmoid Bone

Only the lateral masses of the ethmoid bone that contain the ethmoid air cells and form parts of the medial wall of the orbits and the superior and middle conchae are bony at birth; the rest of the bone consists of cartilage. The perpendicular part forming the upper portion of the nasal septum ossifies during the first year after birth. The two cribriform laminae ossify during the second year and the fibrocartilaginous crista galli between the second and fourth years. These three parts of the ethmoid bone fuse as they ossify and join with the lateral masses during the sixth year after birth.

Maxillae

Each maxilla of the newborn infant is relatively low and broad and its frontal process, which forms the border of the nasal cavity and orbit to abut the frontal bone, is relatively larger than in the adult. The infraorbital foramen is also relatively very large at birth. The alveolar portion contains five large alveoli or fossae containing five large deciduous teeth (Figs. A, B). The bony palate is shallow at birth and is more U-shaped than V-shaped, as it is in the adult. The postnatal growth of the maxilla is in its vertical diameter, due mainly to the enlargement of the maxillary sinus and an increase in the size of the alveolar part. Most of the growth in length is due to the deposition of bone at the posterior end of the maxilla. At birth the greatest anteroposterior length of each maxilla is about 3.0 cm. The distance from the floor of the orbit to the gingival membrane is about 1.0 cm.

Mandible

The newborn mandible consists of lateral bony halves that are united by fibrous tissue at the mandibular suture. The halves fuse at the suture during the end of the first or the beginning of the second year after birth. The body of the mandible at birth is relatively large with its upper two-thirds consisting of alveoli or fossae containing the deciduous and some permanent teeth (Figs. A, B). The rami are short and broad and set at about a 140° angle to the body (Fig. A). The angle is about 120° or less in the adult. The body is longer (3.5 cm) than the ramus (2.0 cm) at birth, whereas they are about the same length in the adult. The body is about 1.0 cm wide at the symphysis. The mandibular notch of the ramus is relatively shallow in the newborn infant and the mandibular foramen is directed more transversely than it is in the adult (Fig. A). The angle of the foramen at birth is 20° to 30° at birth, whereas it is 50° to 70° in adulthood. The maximum thickness of the ramus is 5.0 mm at the level of the foramen.

Teeth

The twenty deciduous teeth at birth consist of only the enamel crowns that are lined internally with dentine around a pulp cavity (Figs. A, B, C). The tiny primordia of all the permanent teeth except those of the second and third molars are also present in the jaws at birth. The crowns of the deciduous teeth are encased in the incomplete bony alveoli of the maxillae and mandible. The oral surfaces of the bony alveoli are covered with the gingival membrane. The formation of the roots is associated with the postnatal eruption of the deciduous teeth that occurs approximately as follows.

(age in months)		*(age in months)*	
6	lower central incisors	14	upper first molars
7	lower lateral incisors	16	lower canines
7½	upper central incisors	18	upper canines
9	upper lateral incisors	20	lower second molars
12	lower first molars	24	upper second molars

The loss of the deciduous teeth precedes the eruption of the associated thirty-two permanent teeth, which occurs approximately as follows.

(age in years)		*(age in years)*	
6–7	lower central incisors, lower first molars, upper first molars	10–12	lower first bicuspids, upper second bicuspids
7–8	lower lateral incisors, upper central incisors	11–12	upper canines, lower second bicuspids
8–9	upper lateral incisors	11–13	lower second molars
9–10	lower canines	12–13	upper second molars
10–11	upper first bicuspids	17–21	upper and lower third (wisdom) molars

Temporal Bones

Each of the temporal bones at birth consists of three parts: the squamous, petrous, and tympanic, separated by sutures. The overall size of the temporal bone of the newborn infant is one-third to one-half that of the adult. However, the petrous part is relatively larger at birth. The mastoid process is absent (Fig. A); it appears as a small projection near the end of the first year after birth but does not really become of noticeable size until two or three years later. The lack of a protective mastoid process exposes the facial nerve passing out of the stylomastoid foramen to injury at birth (e.g. from the blade of obstetric forceps). The styloid process at birth is cartilaginous except for a small osseous granule near its proximal end; it is about 7.0 mm long.

The mandibular fossa of the squamous part of the temporal bone is quite shallow at birth and the articular tubercle is absent. The tympanic part of the temporal bone is in the form of a thin, incomplete bony ring at birth.

The ends of the ring are usually fused with the squamous part of the temporal bone.

At birth the petrous and squamous parts of the temporal bone are usually partially separated by the petrosquamous fissure which opens directly into the mastoid antrum of the middle ear in infants and young children. It is a route for the spread of middle ear infections to the meninges. The fissure closes completely in about 4 percent of children during the first year; however, it is still unclosed in 20 to 40 percent between five and nineteen years of age.

Ear

The external acoustic meatus is relatively long at birth; it is about 16.8 mm, or approximately two-thirds the length it is in the adult (Fig. B). The inner third consists of a tube of dense fibrous membrane that abuts the overhanging lateral surface of the squamous part of the temporal bone. The floor and sides of the inner third become ossified by a lateral extension of the tympanic bone into the membranous tube. The bony roof forms from an outgrowth of a bony shelf from the squamous part of the temporal bone. By the third year after birth a very thin tube of bone is present within the wall of the inner third of the meatus. The wall of the outer two-thirds of the external meatus at birth contains cartilage that is an inner extension of the cartilaginous skeleton of the auricle of the ear medial to the tragus portion. The cartilage does not completely surround the meatus. There is a gap along the upper, anterior part of the meatus that consists of fibrous membrane. There are slits in the cartilage of the anterior wall that abuts the parotid gland. In the adult the inner two-thirds of the S-shaped external meatus is bony and the outer one-third is cartilaginous. In the newborn infant the external meatus is almost straight; it courses inward, downward, and slightly forward. The inclination or slant of the tympanic membrane or eardrum at birth is about 50° to 60°, just as it is in adulthood (Fig. B). Thus the inferior wall or floor of the external meatus is longer than the superior wall or roof. The lumen of the middle part of the external meatus in the newborn infant is very narrow (Fig. B). At birth the lumen is filled with a mass of desquamated epithelial cells and sebaceous secretion, the vernix caseosa.

The newborn middle ear or tympanic cavity is about the same size as in the adult. It is an elongated cavity that is narrow at its midpoint. The anteroposterior and vertical diameters at birth are both about 1 cm. The transverse diameter is about 6 mm at the roof of the cavity, 2 mm at its midpoint, and 4 mm at the floor. As in the adult, the lateral wall consists mainly of the eardrum. The extension of the wall above the eardrum, the epitympanic recess, is well developed at birth as is the mastoid antrum. The bulge on the medial bony wall of the cavity, the promontory, over the basal turn of the cochlea is well marked at birth. The prominence of the facial nerve canal above the promontory is also evident at birth.

The bony openings of the medial wall—the fenestra vestibuli or oval window (2.5 mm long, 1.5 mm wide) and the fenestra tympani or round window (2.0 mm diameter)—are the same size in the newborn infant as in the adult. The auditory ossicles—the malleus or hammer, the incus or anvil, and the stapes or stirrup—reach their adult size as early as the sixth month of fetal life. The eardrum or tympanic membrane has completed its full growth by the time of birth (Fig. B); it is almost circular, with a 1.0-cm diameter. The epithelium of the inner or deep surface of the eardrum, as well as the mucous lining of the middle ear, is ciliated at birth. The mucous lining of the middle ear is also relatively thick and edematous at birth. In 30 percent of newborn infants some nipple-like extensions of the mucous lining (the mastoid cells) extend into the region of the temporal bone immediately posterior to the exit of the facial nerve from the stylomastoid foramen. Some may be as large as 5.0 mm in diameter. The mastoid process, which begins to develop at the end of the first year after birth, usually consists of cancellous bone up to puberty when mastoid air cells begin to invade it. The cavity of the middle ear often contains amniotic fluid and fluid secreted by the respiratory tubes in the newborn infant.

The bony and membranous labyrinths of the inner ear of the newborn infant almost equal those of the adult in size and proportions. The vestibule and semicircular canals increase only about one-tenth in size after birth, and the increase in the size of the cochlea is even less. The inner ear at birth therefore occupies a relatively greater area of the petrous part of the temporal bone. A deep bony fossa along the inferior border of the anterior semicircular canal, the subarcuate fossa, is present at birth (Fig. A). As the petrous part of the temporal bone grows after birth the subarcuate fossa fills in and disappears. Only a small pit may be present at two years of age. The diameter of the internal acoustic meatus at birth is almost as large as that of the adult (Fig. A).

Auditory Tube

During the formation of the human pharynx four pairs of lateral outpocketings or pouches develop. They are homologues of part of the gills of fish. The first pair of pouches is retained in man as dead-end tubes. The distal end of each tube enlarges to become the middle ear cavity. The connection between the pharynx and the middle ear becomes the auditory tube.

The auditory tube in the newborn infant is about 1.7 cm long or half the length it is in the adult. In the middle ear there is a bony canal that is subdivided by a septum (musculotubarii) into two semicanals. The upper semicanal contains the tensor tympani muscle that inserts by a relatively long, narrow tendon onto the manubrium (handle) of the malleus (hammer). The lower semicanal is the middle ear opening of the auditory tube, which at birth is as large as it is in the adult; its diameter is 2.0 mm. However, the pharyngeal opening into the nasal part of the pharynx is relatively smaller at birth (Fig. C); it is a 4.0-mm slit. The elevation of the pharyngeal wall at this opening at birth, the torus tubarius, is also relatively small because of the lack of development of the lymphatic tissue of its mucosa (tubal tonsil) and the fact that the cartilage of the tube does not project into the pharyngeal cavity as far as it does in the adult. After the first year of age the torus tubarius begins to enlarge and in so doing causes the pharyngeal recess behind it to become deeper. The recess is only slightly developed at birth. At birth the pharyngeal opening of the tube is at the level of the floor of the nasal cavity near the junction of the hard and soft palates (Fig. C). After the first year of age the opening is shifted upward and backward so that by the fifth or sixth year it generally lies posterior to the inferior nasal concha, just as it does in the adult.

The bony part of the tube at the middle ear end is relatively longer in the newborn infant. The junction of the bony and cartilaginous parts, the isthmus, is absolutely as well as relatively wider in the newborn infant than it is in the adult. The course of the tube is almost horizontal at birth, whereas starting at the middle ear opening in the adult it passes downward, forward, and medially.

The pharyngeal opening at birth and in later life is closed except when opened by muscle contraction. The cartilaginous part of the auditory tube has cartilage only in the superior and posterior walls because the anterior and inferior walls consist of flexible membrane. The membranous part of the wall at the slit-like pharyngeal opening is elevated by the underlying levator veli palatini muscle. Part of the tensor veli palatini muscle arises from the membranous part of the auditory tube; therefore, when it contracts to tense the soft palate during swallowing, it also opens the auditory tube. The ciliated mucosal lining of the auditory tube at birth continues as the lining of the middle ear cavity including the lining of the eardrum, the bony ossicles, and the developing mastoid air cells. The auditory tube not only serves as a passageway for keeping the proper air pressure on the inner surface of the eardrum for hearing, but it also allows infectious material to pass from the pharynx to the middle ear (otitis media).

Paranasal Sinuses

The paranasal sinuses develop as small diverticula or outpouchings of the mucosal lining of the lateral wall of the nasal cavity. During the third month of fetal development the maxillary sinus appears as a pouch, the neck of which remains small to form the ostium. The distal portion of the pouch enlarges to form the sinus. At birth the maxillary sinus is an elongated sac with an anteroposterior length of 8 to 10 mm and transverse and vertical diameters of 3 to 5 mm each (Fig. B). Between birth and adulthood it becomes three times longer anteroposteriorly and five times greater in height and width. The newborn tubular maxillary sinus does not become pyramidal in shape until after the eruption of the permanent teeth. At birth the floor of the sinus is distinctly above that of the nasal cavity, whereas in the adult it is below it (Fig. B).

During the third month of fetal development the sphenoid sinus appears as a small pouch from the upper posterior part of the nasal cavity that becomes the sphenoethmoidal recess. At birth the sphenoid sinuses occupy a position on either side of an anterior wedge-shaped projection of the body of the sphenoid bone. Although the sinuses do not begin to invade the sphenoid bone until several years after birth, the wedge-shaped anterior end of the bone between them serves as a relatively wide septum for the sinuses. Actually, each sphenoid sinus in the newborn infant has its own extremely thin bony capsule, the sphenoid concha. Except for a difference in the position, the sphenoid conchae are the same as the bony capsules of the ethmoid air cells. Even though the ostium of the sphenoid sinus is small at birth, there may be a wider gap of bone in the wall at the ostium. Each sinus at birth has a diameter of 1.6 to 2.0 mm anteroposteriorly, 2.0 mm laterally, and 2.8 mm vertically. A midsagittal cut through the head of a newborn infant usually goes through the anterior wedge-shaped projection of the body of the sphenoid bone; therefore the sphenoid sinuses on either side of the midline may not be seen at all (Fig. C). At birth the body of the sphenoid bone may have a small craniopharyngeal canal that extends from the pharyngeal surface to the hypophyseal fossa. If the canal is present, it contains a few blood vessels and, rarely, small nodules of hypophyseal gland tissue. The explanation for the presence of the gland tissue is that the canal demarcates the route where the outpouching (Rathke's) of the lining of the embryonic stomodeum (region of future nasopharynx) passed to join the future neurohypophysis of the brain and become the anterior lobes of the hypophysis or pituitary gland. However, the canal may represent a vascular channel that secondarily appeared after the continuity of the future nasopharynx and hypophysis had completely disappeared.

During the latter part of the third and during the fourth fetal month of development the ethmoid cells or sinuses appear as small pouches of the lateral wall of the nasal cavity. At birth, as in adulthood, their number is extremely variable. Even though there may be from three to eighteen cells there is usually a division into three groups—anterior, middle, and posterior. Each group usually shares an ostium. The anterior cells usually open into the anterior part of the hiatus semilunaris of the middle meatus. The middle cells, part of which form the small bulge or bulla of the middle meatus, usually open near the bulla. The posterior cells usually open into the superior meatus. At birth the small air cells have invaded the lateral masses of the ethmoid bone and occupy a position between the nasal cavity and the orbit but do not extend to the level of the floor of the anterior cranial fossa as they do in the adult (Fig. B).

During the end of the third month of fetal development the frontal sinus appears as a pouch from the lateral wall of the nasal cavity in the region of what becomes the anterior part of the semilunar hiatus of the middle meatus, the ethmoidal infundibulum. The sinus may develop as a separate extension of the middle meatus, as one of the original anterior ethmoid cells, or more rarely of the infundibulum. The frontal sinus does not begin to invade the vertical portion of the frontal bone until two years after birth (Fig. A). When it does invade the bone and enlarge, the connection between the sinus and the anterior part of the semilunar hiatus becomes the tubular frontonasal duct.

Since the paranasal sinuses were originally outgrowths of the lining of the developing nasal cavity, the ciliated epithelium of the nasal cavity at birth is continuous with that of each sinus at its opening into the nasal cavity.

Brain

The weight of the brain of the full-term newborn ranges from 300 to 400 gm, with an average of about 350 gm. The brains of newborn males are slightly heavier than those of females. The brain has a jelly-like consistency at birth; about 85 percent of its weight is water (in the early stages of development water constitutes about 50 percent of the extracellular compartment of the brain). The amount of water gradually drops to about 75 percent at around four years of age (at this age water constitutes only 20 percent of the extracellular compartment, with the remainder being intracellular). The total weight of the brain increases from three and a half to four times between birth and maturity. From birth to the end of the first year it increases about two and a half times in weight. At the end of the middle of the fifth year the brain weighs about three times as much as it did at birth. The brain attains its adult weight of 1,100 to 1,700 gm as early as the seventh year but more often by the end of the fifteenth year of age. Throughout this period of weight increase the average weight of the male brain is slightly heavier than the female brain. The extracellular space of the mature brain is only a few angstroms wide. Neurons, neuroglia, and blood vessels are the chief constituents of the mature brain. In the cerebral cortex no neuron is more than 50 microns from a capillary. Protoplasmic astrocytes occupy what is extracellular space in the other organs of the body.

The brain constitutes 10 percent of the body weight at birth, whereas in the adult it is but 2 percent. The weight of the cerebral hemispheres at birth is from 305 to 345 gm, constituting about 93 percent of the entire brain weight. The total increase in the weight of the cerebral hemispheres is 840 gm or more. Nearly one-third of this increase takes place the first nine months after birth, with the other two-thirds occurring by the end of the first two years. The cerebellum weighs from 18 to 20 gm at birth, which is about 5 to 6 percent of the entire weight of the brain. During the period of growth after birth the cerebellum increases about seven times, or nearly twice as much as the brain as a whole. The brain stem weighs about 5 gm in the newborn infant; it weighs from 25 to 28 gm in the adult.

The brain at birth is much larger in relationship to the rest of the head than it is in adulthood (Figs. B, C); its anteroposterior length is 9.0 cm and its transverse width 8.0 cm. The newborn brain occupies a cranial capacity of about 400 cc, whereas the cranial capacity of the adult is from 1,300 to 1,500 cc. The brain has reached 90 percent of its adult size by the fifth year of age; at ten years it has reached 95 percent. Although the frontal lobes of the cerebral hemispheres are relatively large at birth, after birth they grow more than the other parts of the hemispheres.

The sulci of the cerebral hemispheres begin to appear during the fourth fetal month. The general arrangement of the gyri and sulci of the cerebral hemispheres at birth is very similar to that of the adult brain, but the insula is not yet completely covered by adjacent gyri. The lateral sulcus in the newborn infant is more oblique; in the adult it is more horizontal. The central sulcus in the newborn infant is situated a little more forward than it is in the adult.

The ventricles of the brain are relatively larger at birth than in the adult (Figs. B, C). The pons is relatively smaller in the newborn infant than in the adult (Fig. C). The brain stem is more oblique at birth, whereas it is almost vertical in the adult (Fig. C). Therefore, the newborn brain stem has a distinct bend in it as it passes through the foramen magnum to become the spinal medulla (cord) (Fig. C).

The olfactory nerves and the optic chiasma are relatively much larger at birth than in adulthood; the roots of the other cranial nerves are relatively smaller at birth. The basilar artery is relatively smaller in the newborn infant than it is in the adult; it is 1.0 to 1.5 mm wide.

All of the approximately 10 billion neurons of the cerebral cortex of the brain, as well as all of the nerve cells of the rest of the nervous system, are present at birth; in fact they are present as early as the end of the sixth month of fetal life. However, the great majority of cells in the newborn brain are not neurons but neuroglia. Neuroglia continue to proliferate after birth until the full cytological development of the brain is reached at about five years of age, when the number of cells of the cortex approaches 50 billion. During this time it is the neuroglia that increase in number, because the neurons increase in size and in the development of their cell processes rather than in number. Although the dendrites of the cortical neurons begin to develop a few months before birth, they are still quite rudimentary in the newborn infant. It is during the first year after birth that the processes of each cortical neuron develop to establish from 1,000 to 100,000 (average 10,000) connections with other neurons. The neurons of the brain begin to die in increasing numbers in the young adult so that by thirty-five years of age 100,000 brain cells are lost each day.

The cranial nerves of the midbrain, pons, and medulla oblongata begin to become myelinated about the sixth month of fetal life. The motor neurons become myelinated before the sensory neurons. The myelination is associated with the development of the functional capacity of these nerves. Unmyelinated neurons have a long latency, are slow-firing, and fatigue early, whereas myelinated neurons have a short latency, fire rapidly and continuously, and have a long period of activity before fatiguing. Myelination is an orderly process in which the functionally allied systems of neurons are synchronized in an orderly sequence and tempo. At birth the neurons of the brain stem, the basal ganglia, and their cerebellar connecting neurons are myelinated. The neurons of the cerebral hemispheres just begin to become myelinated at birth. Their myelination continues up to puberty. During this period the first to acquire myelin sheaths are the neurons of the olfactory, optic, and acoustic cortical fields and the neurons of the motor cortex (pyramidal cells); the projectional, commissural, and association neurons of the cerebral hemispheres are the last to become myelinated. Myelination of neurons of association areas of the cerebral hemispheres continues through the years of adulthood.

Meninges

The form and relationship of the meninges to the brain and spinal medulla in the newborn infant are generally similar to those in the adult (Fig.

C). At birth the dura mater is closely applied to the skull bones. Its outer layer contains numerous osteoblasts where it is in contact with bone, and it forms the inner layer of the suture membranes and fonticuli. At birth the dura weighs about 22 gm. Its growth is more related to the growth rate of the brain than it is to that of the body because by the seventh year after birth the weight of the dura has increased only about three times.

The overall size of the subarachnoid space, filled with cerebrospinal fluid, is relatively small in the newborn infant because the brain is more closely applied to the skull wall than in the adult. The brain occupies 97.5 percent of the cranial cavity from birth to six years of age. After the sixth year the space between the brain and the cranial wall steadily increases in size until in the adult the brain occupies on the average only 92.5 percent of the cranial cavity. The enlargements of the subarachnoid space (the cisterns) are relatively larger in the infant (Fig. C). The newborn infant has a total of about 10 to 15 ml of cerebrospinal fluid when delivered vaginally, or 30 ml when delivered by cesarian section. The adult total is about 100 to 150 ml of cerebrospinal fluid.

The dural venous sinuses at birth are similar to those of the adult (Fig. C). However, the arachnoid villi present at birth in the superior sagittal sinus are microscopic in size. The lateral lacunae of the superior sagittal sinus are either absent or microscopic. The great cerebral vein in the newborn infant, by virtue of its brain stem branches, is attached to the brain stem that is firmly bound in position by its cranial nerves to the base of the skull. The other end of the great vein is attached to the falx cerebri and the tentorium cerebelli where it joins the straight sinus (Fig. C). The straight sinus end of the great vein is quite mobile because the falx and tentorium are continuous with the dura that is firmly attached to the calvarial bones. Due to the wide flexible sutures and the fonticuli, the calvarial bones can be displaced to the extent that they actually overlap each other at the sutures during parturition. The skull "molding" occurring during the delivery of the head at childbirth exerts tension on the great cerebral vein. The tensional stress may be severe enough to rupture the great vein or even tear the tentorium and rupture the straight sinus. The great vein is about 8.0 mm long and 4.0 mm wide.

Hypophysis (Pituitary Gland)

The hypophysis at birth weighs about 0.1 gm or about one-sixth the weight of the adult gland (Fig. C). The birth weight of the gland increases by a half during the first year after birth. At seven years of age it is about one-half the adult weight and at the end of puberty its postnatal growth is nearing completion when it weighs about 0.5 gm.

The hypophysis at birth has an anteroposterior length of about 2.5 mm, a transverse length of 4.0 mm, and a vertical length of 3.0 mm. In the adult the anteroposterior average length is 9.0 mm, the transverse 14.0 mm, and the vertical 6.0 mm. Throughout postnatal life the average relative size and weight of the hypophysis are always distinctly greater in females than in males.

The hypophysis becomes functional under the influence of the hypothalamus long before birth. Gonadotrophins are produced as early as the ninth week of development. Adrenocorticotrophic hormone is released between the eighth and ninth weeks and thyrotrophic hormone by four and a half months of development. Growth and lactogenic hormones are produced in small amounts by the fetal hypophysis at the tenth week of development.

Eye

The eyeball is relatively large at birth (Fig. B). The average weight of the eyeball in the newborn infant is from 2.5 to 3.0 gm. The weight increases about three times between birth and adulthood. In contrast, the weight of the body increases during this time over twenty times. The anteroposterior diameter of the newborn eyeball is about 16.4 mm, the horizontal diameter 16.0 mm, and the vertical diameter 15.4 mm. In the adult these same measurements are 23.8, 24.4, and 23.7 mm respectively. Although the newborn eyeball is smaller than that of the adult, its shape and proportions are very similar. The cornea of the newborn infant is relatively slightly larger than that of the adult and its curvature is less pronounced.

The shape of the lens at birth is about the same as in adulthood. The thickness of the newborn lens is from 3.5 to 4.0 mm and the equatorial diameter from 6.0 to 7.0 mm. From birth to adulthood the equatorial diameter increases between a third and a fourth. The newborn lens is relatively more flexible than that of the young adult; therefore, in sectioned newborn eyeballs, where the lens is released from the tension of its attachments, it appears more spherical. During the growth of the eyeball after birth there is a slight shift in the position of the insertions of the extrinsic muscles.

The optic nerve increases more than one-half in diameter during the first year after birth. At the end of the first year the diameter is about the same as that of the adult nerve. Much of this increase is due to the myelination of the one million optic neurons that occurs mainly during the first three weeks after birth. As in the adult, the optic nerve curves slightly in its course through the orbit. The dural sheath surrounding the nerve is relatively flexible, due to the underlying subarachnoid space containing cerebrospinal fluid.

The lacrimal gland is relatively much larger at birth than in adulthood. At birth the gland is about one-third its adult weight. The amount of tear secretion is relatively small, to some degree because the functional part of the gland consists of narrow thick-walled ducts separated by large amounts of connective tissue. The nasolacrimal duct, which drains the tear secretion from the lacrimal sac to the inferior meatus of the nasal cavity, is relatively much shorter and wider at birth than it is in adulthood. The bony nasolacrimal canal that surrounds part of the nasolacrimal duct in the adult is only a foramen in the newborn infant.

Although the orbits at birth are much greater in size relative to the rest of the skull than in the adult, they are much smaller relative to the size of the adult eyeball (Fig. B). Almost the entire eyeball is unprotected laterally by orbital bone. Therefore there is relatively less orbital fat at birth than in adulthood where it fills the larger intervals between the orbit and its contained structures. Orbital fat is only slightly diminished in extreme cases of emaciation. Female adults have larger eyeballs in proportion to their body weight and in relation to the size of the orbits than male adults. At birth the orbit at its margin is 1.9 cm high and 2.3 cm wide. Its maximum depth is about 3.0 cm.

Oral Cavity and Tongue

The newborn oral cavity is only a potential one when the mouth is closed because the tongue comes into contact with the gums (gingivae) laterally and with the roof of the mouth above (Fig. C). The hard palate is short, wide, and only slightly arched at birth, whereas it is deeply arched both anteroposteriorly and tranversely in the adult (Fig. C). Usually it is corrugated by a series of five to six irregular transverse folds that may be entirely obliterated or broken up into mound-like elevations before adulthood. They assist the newborn infant in holding the nipple during suckling. A small conical projection, the incisive papilla, is present at the middle of the anterior margin of the palate at birth.

The tongue of the newborn infant is relatively short and broad (Fig. C). With the mouth closed it is about 4.0 cm long, 2.5 cm wide, and 1.0 cm thick. The sulcus terminalis, that demarcates the division between the oral and future pharyngeal portions, is quite evident. The foramen cecum, which demarcates where the outgrowth of the embryonic pharynx occurred to become the thyroid gland, is usually a distinct pit on the newborn tongue (Fig. C). All the types of lingual papillae of the adult are present before birth. Taste buds are present on the vallate, foliate, and fungiform papillae, and in the epithelium of the foramen cecum at birth. Of all the tastes, the newborn infant has an increased suckling response only to sweet. The lymphoid follicles of the lingual tonsil begin to form at birth.

The entire surface of the newborn tongue is within the oral cavity, just as it is in an adult monkey or ape (Fig. C). Of all the air-breathing vertebrates, only in man does the posterior third of the tongue descend into the neck after birth to become a part of the anterior wall of the pharynx. The descent begins gradually during the first year after birth and is essentially completed by the fourth or fifth year of age. Since the tongue is attached directly to the epiglottis of the larynx, the opening of the larynx is directly below the oral cavity before the tongue descends. The high position of the epiglottis at birth allows it to make direct contact with the soft palate (Fig. C). When the structures of the oral cavity of the newborn infant assume their position for suckling, three cleft-like spaces are formed through which fluids pass into the pharynx. One space is a median cavity that lies between the tongue and hard palate. Passing posteriorly the median cavity divides into two channels in the isthmus faucium region, one on each side of the approximated soft palate and epiglottis. The isthmus region is bounded laterally by the palatoglossal arch and the palatopharyngeal arch with the palatine tonsil between the two. The other two spaces are lateral arcuate cavities between the gums (gingivae) that are present on each side of the oral cavity when the infant suckles, because the upper and lower gums are not approximated during the act of suckling. The medial walls of these lateral cavities are formed by the tongue, and the lateral walls by the cheeks. Fluids pass from each of these lateral cavities into the isthmus clefts on the same side of the oral cavity, between the arches and tonsil laterally and the approximated soft palate and epiglottis medially, to get to the pharynx. As fluid passes from the median and lateral cavities through the narrowed isthmus clefts on each side of the approximated epiglottis and soft palate, the larynx is elevated so that its opening is above the level of the isthmus clefts conveying fluid into the pharynx. The elevation of the larynx also directs the opening of the larynx into the nasopharynx so that the infant can breathe freely while fluid is passing into its pharynx.

The newborn infant is an obligate nose breather. Obstruction of the nasal airway by any means produces an extremely stressful reaction and the infant will submit to breathing through the mouth only when the point of suffocation is reached. The descent of the larynx into the neck during early childhood results in the lowering of the opening of the larynx into the most inferior part of the pharynx. Compared to the anatomy of the newborn infant this is an undesirable arrangement; if material lodges in the pharynx it blocks the flow of air to the larynx.

Buccal Fat Pad

The buccal fat pad in the newborn infant is a circumscribed mass of adipose tissue that lies in the space between the buccinator and masseter muscles and is covered externally by the facial muscles and superficial fascia. The fat pad is continuous with adipose tissue surrounding the temporalis muscle and coronoid process of the mandible deep to the bony zygomatic arch. The buccal fat pad is enclosed within its own capsule of fibrous connective tissue. Its function in the infant was believed to be the distribution of atmospheric pressure and the prevention of the drawing in of the cheek and buccinator muscle between the gums during the act of suckling, thus it was also known as the suctorial or sucking fat pad. The buccal fat persists in adulthood and is only slightly diminished in extreme cases of emaciation.

Salivary Glands

The relative weight of the salivary glands as a whole is about the same in the newborn infant and the adult. However, the parotid gland in the infant is proportionately a little lighter while the submandibular and the sublingual are a little heavier. The parotid at birth weighs about 1.8 gm, the submandibular 0.84 gm, and the sublingual 0.42 gm. Each of these glands increases in weight about three times during the first six months after birth and five times during the first two years. All the salivary glands acquire the adult histological characteristics during the first two years after birth.

The parotid gland in the newborn infant is rounder than in the adult. It lies wedged in the space between the masseter muscle and the ear. During early childhood the gland gradually grows over the surface of the parotid duct until the final form of the adult gland is acquired. The parotid duct pierces the buccinator muscle to open into the oral cavity.

The topography of the submandibular and sublingual glands is similar in the newborn infant and the adult. The deep portion of the submandibular gland is usually continuous with the sublingual gland in the newborn infant, whereas in the adult the two are usually separate.

Nasal Cavities

The nasal cavities of the newborn infant are low, broad, and relatively long (Figs. B, C). The height of each cavity is 18.0 to 19.0 mm. This height increases nearly one-half during the first year after birth. At the seventh year it is about double and in the adult from two and one-half to three times that of the newborn infant. The anteroposterior length of the floor of each nasal cavity at its base is about 7.0 mm. It is about 9.5 mm by the fifth year of age and about double that of the newborn infant at adulthood.

The nasal conchae are all differentiated before birth and one or all of the three supreme conchae may still be present at birth. Even when they do not appear to be present, the bony skeleton of a supreme concha lies deep to the mucosal covering of the superior concha. The lower margin of the inferior concha is often in contact with the floor of the newborn nasal cavity.

The nasal septum is long and low in the newborn infant and, except for the vomer bone, is composed entirely of cartilage. The perpendicular plate of the ethmoid bone forming the upper part of the septum ossifies during the first year after birth. The septum is straight at birth, whereas it is frequently deviated in the adult (Fig. B).

The height and width of each of the choanae or posterior nares are about equal (5.0 to 7.0 mm) at birth. They double in size by the end of two years of age. The height increases much more rapidly than the width so that the ratio between height and width, which is about 1:1 at birth, is about 3:2 at three years and 2:1 in the adult. The nasal cavities usually are filled with fluid and mucus at birth.

Tonsils

At birth the posterior part of the roof of the nasal part of the pharynx has a small median pit from which a series of folds radiates forward and laterally. The pharyngeal tonsil is formed by the infiltration of these folds with poorly defined masses of lymphoid cells shortly before birth. During the first year after birth the lymphoid tissue is greatly increased and definite follicles with germinal centers are formed. The pharyngeal tonsil (adenoids) reaches its maximum development during the sixth year of age. At that time it normally occupies half of what had been the cavity of the nasopharynx before its enlargement. When it is abnormally enlarged from chronic infection it forms a sufficient block of the nasopharynx to induce mouth-breathing in the child. Usually associated with this enlargement is an abnormal enlargement of the lymphoid tissue of the torus tubarius at the ostia of the adjacent auditory tubes (tubal tonsil) that can block the tubes and result in deafness and/or middle ear infection (otitis media).

Involution of the pharyngeal tonsil begins at six or seven years of age and is completed before puberty; however, it may persist to adulthood.

At birth, as in adulthood, the palatine tonsils are lodged in the tonsillar fossa in the region between the palatoglossal arch and the palatopharyngeal arch (isthmus faucium). The tonsil lies higher in the tonsillar fossa at birth than in adulthood. Its greatest length at birth of 5.0 mm is in the horizontal anteroposterior plane. Its vertical length is about 3.5 mm. As the tonsil descends slightly in position during the second and third years after birth, the greatest length shifts to the vertical plane. Although lymphoid tissue is located in the palatine tonsils in the six-month fetus, it is not until birth or shortly thereafter that definite lymphoid nodules appear. The newborn tonsil weighs about 0.75 gm. Usually the palatine tonsils begin to atrophy between the fifth year of age and puberty. The supratonsillar fossa may become the site of a deep-seated infection.

The palatine tonsils along with the pharyngeal tonsil, tubal tonsils, and lingual tonsil form the tonsillar ring (Waldeyer's) that guards the entrance of the digestive and respiratory systems from infection.

Pharynx

The pharynx in the newborn infant is about 4 cm in length, or one-third as long as it is in the adult (Fig. C). The roof of the nasal part is in contact with the sphenoid and occipital bones and their intervening synchondrosis (Fig. C). The posterior wall of the entire pharynx abuts the cervical vertebral column (Fig. C). The lateral walls of the entire pharynx are made up almost completely of the pharyngeal constrictor muscles. Anteriorly, the nasal part of the newborn pharynx is continuous with the choanae of the nasal cavities, and the oral part of the pharynx is continuous with the oral cavity (Fig. C). After the posterior third of the tongue descends into the neck to become permanently situated there, about four years after birth, the posterior third of the tongue forms the anterior wall of the oral part of the pharynx, below the opening of the oral cavity. Anteriorly, the laryngeal part of the newborn pharynx is continuous with the inlet of the larynx immediately below the opening into the oral cavity (Fig. C). After the descent of the tongue into the neck, the inlet of the larynx is located in a much lower position in the laryngeal part of the pharynx.

At birth the pharynx at rest extends inferiorly to the level of the fifth or the lower level of the sixth cervical vertebra posteriorly and the cricoid cartilage anteriorly (Fig. C). The inferior extent of the pharynx is at about the same vertebral level as in the adult because, as the pharynx increases in length, the growth of the cervical vertebral column keeps pace with it.

At birth the shape of the pharynx resembles that of an adult ape. The nasal part is a narrow tube about 20 mm long that curves very gradually downward to join the oral part without any sharp line of demarcation (Fig. C). By five years of age the posterior walls of the nasal and oral parts meet at an oblique angle. At the time of puberty, as in the adult, they join almost at a right angle.

In the newborn infant the location of the laryngeal opening into the pharynx, immediately below the opening of the oral cavity into the pharynx, is the same as that of the adult monkey and ape, which greatly limits their phonetic repertoire. The newborn human and adult ape could not produce the articulate speech of language even if they had the necessary central nervous system connections. It is necessary that the laryngeal opening into the pharynx be located at a much lower level than it is in the newborn infant or ape so that the air column emitted from the larynx passes through a relatively long expanse of pharynx before it enters the oral cavity. This allows the pharyngeal and certain tongue muscles to make rapid alterations in the size and shape of the pharynx so that what are known as formant frequencies are produced. These frequencies, along with the activity of the anterior parts of the tongue, the jaws, and the lips, result in the production of the sounds of articulate speech. The nasal cavity is not necessary for articulate speech and the larynx serves only as the source of fundamental frequencies. In an adult, whose larynx is surgically removed, the vibrations of the walls of the esophagus and pharynx produced by belching air from the stomach can substitute for those produced by the vocal folds of the larynx. Thus the development of the pharynx after birth, as well as the development of the proper neural connections, is necessary for the production of the articulate speech of language.

The opening of the auditory tube into the nasal part of the pharynx is described with the auditory tube.

Larynx

The larynx of the newborn infant is about 2.0 cm in length. Its maximum width, at the level of the upper margin of the thyroid cartilage, is almost equal to its length. The absolute dimensions of the larynx at birth are approximately one-third those of the adult; relatively, it is larger than in the adult (Figs. B, C). The thyroid cartilage in the newborn infant is broader and shorter and lies closer to the hyoid bone than it does in the adult. Also, neither the laryngeal prominence (Adam's apple) nor the superior notch of the thyroid cartilage is as marked as it is in the adult. The cricoid cartilage at birth is, in general, the same shape as that of the adult (Fig. C). The cavity of the larynx is short and funnel-shaped at birth. The vocal folds (cords) are from 4.0 to 4.5 mm in length and are relatively shorter than in later childhood and in the adult. The newborn ventricle of the larynx is relatively small but the laryngeal saccule is often of considerable size.

The subglottic cavity below the level of the vocal folds extends backward as well as downward in the newborn infant, whereas it is almost vertical in older children and in the adult (Fig. C). This inclination of the axis of the lower part of the laryngeal cavity is important in connection with the intubation of the young infant for administering an anesthetic. The tube used for intubating an infant not only must be small but also be properly shaped for the airway and introduced correctly. The mucosal lining of the infant larynx readily becomes edematous when irritated, to the point that it may obstruct the flow of air.

Sexual differences of the larynx appear about the third year after birth. The larynx becomes longer and larger in boys; the angle between the laminae of the cartilage becomes more pronounced in girls. The sexual differences are accentuated during puberty when the male larynx increases in size much more than that of the female. The angle of union of the thyroid laminae is about 90° in men and about 120° in women. This difference is related to the much larger laryngeal prominence (Adam's apple) in men than in women. The vocal folds (cords) become longer and thicker in the male during puberty to cause a distinct change in the sound of his voice.

At birth, with the larynx at rest, the upper border of the epiglottis is at the level of the second or third cervical vertebra (Fig. C). With the larynx elevated, it is at the first cervical vertebral level. The larynx descends in the neck after birth along with the descent of the tongue. The descent and its importance for speech are described with the pharynx. In the adult the upper border of the epiglottis is at the level of the lower part of the third or the upper part of the fourth cervical vertebra. The vertical length of the epiglottic cartilage at birth is 1.2 cm.

Hyoid Bone

At birth the position of the hyoid bone is relatively much higher in the neck than it is in adulthood (Figs. A, C). Its lesser cornu is attached by the stylohyoid ligament to the styloid process, which is more horizontally inclined than it usually is in the adult. The hyoid bone is closely attached below by the thyrohyoid membrane to the thyroid cartilage (Fig. C); after birth it therefore descends along with the larynx to a lower position in the neck. A horizontal groove is present along the body of the hyoid of the newborn that demarcates its double origin during early development. The upper half of the body, the lesser cornua, stylohyoid ligaments, and stapes of the middle ear arise from mesenchymal tissue of the second embryonic branchial arch. The lower half of the body and greater cornua arise from the mesenchymal tissue of the third embryonic branchial arch. At birth a small ossification center is present in the body of the chiefly cartilaginous hyoid (Figs. A, C). The vertical height of the body is 5.0 mm and its thickness is 2.0 mm. The distance from the tip of one greater cornu passing along the body to the tip of the other greater cornu measures 3.0 cm.

Thyroid and Parathyroid Glands

The thyroid gland at birth usually resembles more the fetal type than it does the adult type, by virtue of having a relatively long narrow isthmus connecting relatively large lobes that are not in intimate contact with the upper part of the trachea as they are in the adult (Figs. B, C). The thyroid gland usually weighs from 1.5 to 2.5 gm at birth; it weighs about 15.0 gm at puberty. The shape of the gland varies too considerably to arrive at meaningful dimensions for the first two years after birth. The vertical length of a lateral lobe at birth is about 1.0 cm, its width about 4.0 mm, and its greatest thickness about 2.5 mm. As with the larynx at birth, the thyroid gland is relatively large, especially in relationship to the small trachea. At the end of two years after birth the gland is about half the size it is in the adult. Colloid is present in the gland at birth; it appears in the follicles at about the third month of fetal life. Thyroxin is present in the glands by four and a half months of development.

The parathyroid glands, usually embedded in the posterior aspect of the lobes of the thyroid gland, are as variable in number, position, and size at birth as they are in adulthood. At birth the upper two of the usual four parathyroid glands are about 2.9 mm long, 1.9 mm wide, and 1.2 mm thick; the lower two 3.0 mm long, 2.4 mm wide, and 1.4 mm thick. The parathyroid glands double in size between birth and puberty. Parathyroid hormone is first produced by the glands during the twelfth week of fetal life.

Upper Limbs

The upper limbs of the newborn infant are long in relationship to the trunk and lower limbs (Fig. A). The upper limbs are approximately the same length as the lower ones (16.5 cm or 6½ inches) and more developed at birth. However, the upper limbs are proportionately much shorter than those of the adult. Although the hands extend almost to the same level of the upper thighs as they do in the adult, the thorax, abdomen, and especially the pelvis are proportionately much larger in the adult. The arm of the newborn upper limb is proportionately shorter in relationship to the forearm than it is in the adult.

The cubital vein at the elbow, which is so commonly injected for diagnostic and therapeutic purposes in children and adults, is very small in the newborn infant. Its diameter is less than 1.0 mm.

The fingers are usually relatively long and slender in the newborn infant. The middle finger is about 2.2 cm long and 6.0 mm wide at its base. As early as the fourth month of fetal development, epidermal ridges are present in the skin of the palm and fingers which will serve to increase the friction of the skin surface after birth. In each fetus the lines of epidermal ridges form distinct patterns (fingerprints) unlike those of any other human being.

In the dissection of the newborn infant it is less difficult than in the adult to determine that there are four distinct palmar interosseous muscles in the hand instead of the three officially recognized ones. The officially recognized deep head of the flexor pollicis brevis muscle is actually the first palmar interosseous because it has a different origin and innervation than the superficial head. Its innervation is the same as that of the other palmar interosseous muscles, the deep branch of the ulnar nerve.

The newborn hand has a relatively strong grasp. In a full-term newborn the fingernails may extend slightly beyond the tips of the fingers. Once the nails become air-dried they are firm enough to inflict damage to the eyes and skin of the face as the newborn grasps about aimlessly with its hand.

Except for the ossification center of the head of the humerus, only primary ossification centers are present in the skeleton of the upper limb at birth (Fig. A). The primary ossification center of the clavicle appears during the sixth week of fetal life. It is the first bone to ossify in the entire body. The primary ossification centers of the carpal bones of the wrist do not appear until the early part of the first year after birth. The last to appear is in the pisiform shortly before puberty. The ossification centers appear earlier in the female than in the male and are usually bilaterally symmetrical.

Thorax

The thorax of the newborn infant has the form of a truncated cone with a broad base that is slightly flattened anteroposteriorly (Figs. A, B, C). The posterior wall of the thorax in the newborn infant is as long in proportion to the trunk as it is in the adult, but the sternum is much shorter both in proportion to the thoracic vertebral column and to the trunk. The superior margin of the sternum at birth lies opposite the body of the second thoracic vertebra, and the tip of the xiphoid process is at the level of the lower part of the ninth or the upper part of the tenth thoracic vertebra (Fig. C). In the newborn infant the ribs are less curved and their position is more horizontal than in the adult; therefore, the position of the upper margin of the sternum and the tip of the xiphoid process in the adult are at one or one and one-half vertebral levels lower than in the newborn infant. The horizontal circumference of the thorax at the level of the mammary glands, with respiration completely established, is 34.0 to 35.0 cm. Before the first inspiration of air this measurement is about 30.0 cm and after the first breath it is 31.2 cm. Thus it is several days after birth before the lungs acquire their full expansion and the maximum circumference of the thorax is attained. The thorax of the newborn infant appears almost circular in cross section because of the relatively greater anteroposterior diameter.

At birth the sternum is a flexible strip of cartilage 5.0 cm long containing a variable number of ossification centers (Figs. A, C). The manubrium of the sternum usually contains one main center and possibly one or two small ones situated below the main one. The body of the sternum consists of four segments. The upper segments usually contain a single center, whereas the lower segments are generally paired. The ossification of the fourth and lowest segments begins at or shortly after birth. The ossification center of the xiphoid appears during the third year after birth. The primary ossification centers of the ribs appear in the body of the rib early in the fourth month of fetal development. The secondary ossification centers for the head and tubercle of the rib appear at about the time of puberty.

Breathing is essentially a diaphragmatic and abdominal-wall muscular activity in the newborn. The thorax offers little more than a relatively fixed chamber in which the diaphragm's descent and ascent induce the movement of air in and out of the lungs. Since at birth the skeleton of the thorax consists of so much cartilage, it is quite flexible. It may be sufficiently yielding that when negative pressure develops during inspiration the thorax collapses inwardly with each breath, especially in the premature infant.

Thymus

The average weight of the thymus gland at birth is 10.0 gm. The weight of the gland increases steadily from birth to puberty and then it slowly decreases until old age. At puberty it weighs 30.0 gm, in the young adult 18.6 gm, and in the old adult 12.5 gm. The thymus constitutes 0.42 percent of the body weight at birth and 0.03 to 0.05 percent in adulthood.

The thymus becomes both relatively and absolutely longer in childhood, while the width and thickness undergo only a little absolute increase and are relatively reduced. It reaches its greatest relative size at about two years of age. The form of the thymus varies at birth; the most common form is the bilobar type (Figs. B, C). Another common form is the trilobar type in which the gland is composed of two inferior lateral masses and a median superior one. Other forms are those in which no definite lobation is evident.

The length of the gland at birth varies from 4.0 to 6.0 cm, the width from 2.5 to 5.0 cm, and the thickness about 1.0 cm. The cervical portion of the gland is usually a tongue-like process that may extend as high as the lower margin of the thyroid gland. It rests on the anterior surface of the trachea and the carotid sheaths (Figs. B, C). Its anterior surface is covered by the sternohyoid and sternothyroid muscles and their fascia. The thoracic portion of the thymus at birth is covered by the upper half of the sternum and generally by the first three costal cartilages. Its vertical extent corresponds to the first four or five thoracic vertebrae. The posterior surface of the thymus abuts the great vessels of the superior mediastinum, the upper part of the thoracic part of the trachea, and the upper part of the anterior surface of the heart (Figs. B, C). The lower end of the right lobe at birth is commonly tucked into a cavity between the right side of the ascending aorta and the right lung, anterior to the superior vena cava.

After respiration is established the gland becomes more elongated and the right lobe extends more inferiorly over the right ventricle (Figs. B, C). The relationship of the posterior surface of the thymus to the left brachiocephalic vein is a very intimate one at birth (Fig. C). The vein may be partially embedded in the gland substance. Anteriorly, the thymus in the newborn infant is in contact with the endothoracic fascia covering the deep surface of the sternum and the internal thoracic vessels, and laterally with the pleura. At birth the thickest part of the gland lies immediately above the base of the heart and not at the superior thoracic aperture (Fig. C).

The thymus gradually becomes longer and narrower in infancy and childhood. As it elongates it extends downward and the cervical portion becomes less noticeable.

The thymic tissue consists primarily of lymphocytes. After puberty the thymic tissue gradually becomes infiltrated with fat. The gland produces immunologically potent cells (thymocytes) that play a vital role in the development of the immunological system of the body which is in an immature state at the time of birth. The thymus is necessary for the development of the white pulp of the spleen.

Trachea

The average length of the trachea in the full-term infant is about 4.0 cm; the length in the adult is about three times that in the newborn infant. As in the adult, the trachea in the newborn infant is broader above than below and its width from side to side is slightly greater (5.0 mm) than from front to back (3.6 mm) (Figs. B, C). The widest diameter in the adult is 18.0 mm. The trachea is relatively small in relation to the larynx at birth (Figs. B, C). The walls of the trachea are relatively thick at birth and the total number of sixteen to twenty tracheal cartilages is present before birth. The tracheal cartilages and the anular ligaments separating them grow at the same rate during childhood. After puberty the increase in the length of the trachea is the result chiefly of an increase in breadth of the anular ligaments. Therefore, the tracheal cartilages are relatively much closer together than they are in the adult. As in the adult, the posterior membranous part of the newborn trachea constitutes about one-fourth of the circumference of the trachea. The trachealis smooth muscle of the membranous part may be as thick in the newborn infant as it is in the adult. The majority of the tracheal glands of the mucosa are present at birth.

The ability of the newborn trachea to resist external compression is very weak—about a third that of a year-old infant, a fourth that of a five-year-old child, and a sixth that of an adult. The elasticity of the trachea is considerable up to puberty when it decreases in amount.

The upper limit of the trachea in the newborn infant lies at the level of the sixth cervical vertebra, with the head held erect and the larynx at rest (Fig. C). This relationship is maintained to adulthood chiefly because, as the cervical vertebral column grows, the larynx descends to a relatively lower level in the neck.

At birth, the bifurcation of the trachea to form the bronchi is at the level of the third or fourth thoracic vertebra, whereas in adulthood it is at the level of the lower border of the fifth thoracic vertebra (Figs. B, C).

Bronchi and Alveoli

As in the adult, the right main bronchus in the newborn infant is wider, shorter, and more vertical than the left main bronchus (Fig. B). The right main bronchus at birth is 4.6 × 5.0 mm wide and 9.0 mm long, whereas the left is 3.9 × 4.1 mm wide and 21.0 mm long. The basic branching of the bronchi into the bronchopulmonary segments of the lungs, as well as the segmental branching of the pulmonary vessels, is already established in the five- to six-week-old fetus. However, the number of bronchioles and alveoli within bronchopulmonary segments continues to increase until a short time before puberty, when the last new alveoli form. At birth there is a total of about 25 million alveoli in each lung; there are about 300 million in each mature lung. Before the newborn takes its first breath of air the terminal bronchioles and alveoli are not collapsed but are normally filled with fluid, cellular debris, and glandular secretions. Some of the fluid is amniotic fluid;

however, nearly all of it is produced by the lining of the respiratory tubes, as much as 120 ml an hour. Most of this fluid that issues from the lungs passes through the nasopharynx into the nasal cavities. It then passes out through the nares to mix with the amniotic fluid. There is a greater amount of fluid in the respiratory tubes of a newborn infant delivered by cesarian section than in one delivered vaginally. There is a significant increase in the flow of lymph from the lungs after the onset of breathing at birth to aid the vascular system in the clearance of intra-alveolar fluid from the lungs. The presence of fluid in the alveoli before birth is related to an active pulmonary vascular resistance that is present before birth. When air-breathing begins, the hormone bradykinin, formed in the umbilical cord blood and by the granular leukocytes in the lungs, induces a 90 percent reduction in the vascular resistance. The pulmonary blood flow increases by 200 percent or more.

In order for the alveoli to expand and fill with air when the infant starts to breathe, the surface tension has to be reduced. The reduction is brought about by a surface-acting material, or surfactant, secreted by a specific type of cell lining the alveoli. The phospholipid, lecithin, is an important component of the surfactant that reduces the surface tension of the alveoli to between 5 and 7 dynes. (Surface tension is measured in dynes. Water is 72 dynes and when mixed with commercial detergents the tension is reduced to about 20 dynes.) The first breath of life requires very high intrathoracic pressures to expand the lungs with air. On expiration after the first breath the lungs retain considerable residual air, up to 40 percent of the total lung volume. With subsequent breaths, inspiratory pressures are therefore far lower. It is the presence of surfactant in the alveolar lining that keeps enough residual air in the lungs on expiration to prevent alveolar collapse at each breath. For this reason, in a premature infant lacking surfactant, every breath requires almost as much effort as the first. The surfactant not only reduces surface tension but also lines the alveoli to protect the alveolar cells from the direct exposure to oxygen, which is toxic. The surfactant first appears in the fetus at about six to seven months of development. The half-life of the surfactant is 24 hours; therefore it must be continuously produced. In a premature infant less than 32 weeks of age, or less than 1,000 gm in weight, there is a 50 percent chance that surfactant production is insufficient and hyaline membrane disease will develop to cause the infant's death.

Lungs and Pleura

In the newborn infant after full respiration has been attained, the weight of each lung is about 30 gm. In the adult it is twenty times that of the newborn, or 600 gm. The ratio of the weight of the lungs to the weight of the body at birth is 1:70, whereas in adulthood it is about 1:40. The birth weight is doubled during the first six months and is tripled by the end of the first year after birth. From the time the lung buds form in the embryo up to adulthood, the right lung is larger than the left. In the newborn infant the lungs are relatively shorter and broader than those of the adult (Fig. B). This difference between the infant and adult is related to the differences in the shape and capacity of the thorax. The height of the medial surface of the lung at rest is about 2.5 cm. The anteroposterior length of the base is about 4.0 cm, and the greatest transverse width of the base is 2.2 cm.

There is very little change in the skeletal relations of the lungs from birth to adulthood. The relationship of the fissures and lobes to the bony thorax are about the same as in the adult (Fig. B). After respiration begins the apices of the lungs in the newborn infant lie 5 to 8 mm above the level of the superior margin of the sternum and the inferior margins lie at the level of the eleventh rib posteriorly.

In the full-term infant, as in the adult, the lungs do not fill the entire potential pleural cavity, especially the costodiaphragmatic pleural recesses. The reflections of the two pleurae forming the costomediastinal recesses anteriorly are quite variable. They may not approximate each other at any point along the midline. When they do not, a portion of the anterior surface of the thymus gland, along with the pericardium is in direct contact with the endothoracic fascia lining the sternum.

The respiratory rate of a full-term infant is 40 to 44 breaths per minute, with extremes under normal resting circumstances of 20 to 100. The normal resting rate of an adult male is about 12 breaths per minute.

Heart

The cardiac output of blood in a full-term infant is about 550 ml per minute and the blood pressure is 80 over 46. The cardiac output is greater in proportion to the body weight than the output of the adult heart which is about 3 liters per minute. Thus the heart is relatively large at birth and from then on grows less rapidly (Figs. B, C). The infant's pulse is normally quite irregular. The rate is about 65 per minute shortly after the heart first starts to beat at the end of the third week of embryonic development. Near term the fetal pulse rate is 150 per minute. At birth it is about 180; around ten minutes after birth it drops to about 170. From fifteen minutes to an hour after birth it drops to between 120 and 140. From six months to one year of age the pulse rate is between 113 and 127 per minute; it is about 100 at the end of the first year. The normal adult rate is 70 to 72 for men and 72 to 82 for women.

The weight of the heart at birth is about 20 gm. This is increased five times during the first six years after birth, ten times by puberty, and fifteen times by twenty years of age. At birth and during the first year after birth the weight of the ventricles compared to that of the atria is 4–5:1. From the first year on, the ventricles grow more rapidly than the atria so that the weight relation between the two is a little less than 6:1 in later childhood and a little more than 6:1 in adulthood. Even though the left ventricle weighs about a fourth more than the right one at birth, there is normally a right ventricular functional preponderance during the first two or three months after birth. The left ventricle grows so rapidly after birth that by the end of the second year it weighs twice as much as the right. From puberty until middle age the left ventricle is about twice the weight of the right. Since no new cardiac muscle fibers form after birth, the postnatal growth is an increase in muscle fiber size and not in their number.

The differences in postnatal development of the right and left ventricles is also reflected by the changes in thickness of the lateral walls. At birth the average thickness of the lateral walls of the right and left ventricles is about equal (5 mm). By the end of the third month after birth the left is distinctly thicker. At the end of the second year the wall of the left ventricle is twice as thick, and by puberty it is three times as thick as the right.

In the full-term infant in which respiration has been established the heart lies midway between the crown of the head and the lower level of the buttocks (Fig. B). The heart is much larger at birth in relation to the thorax and lungs than it is in the adult (Fig. B). As in the adult, the greatest part of the anterior surface of the heart is formed by the right atrium and the right ventricle. The twist of the heart on its axis, due to differential growth, shifts its original right side to an anterior position and its left side to a posterior one as early as the third month of fetal development. The bare area of the pericardium, not covered by pleura, is smaller in the infant after the first postnatal week when the lungs have acquired their full expansion. The thymus at birth usually covers the anterior surface of the right atrium and may even extend a little over the base of the right ventricle (Figs. B, C). The topographic position of the valves of the newborn heart and great vessels is shown in Figure B. The foramen ovale lies with its long axis in the median plane of the body at the level of the third intercostal space. It is almost exactly in the frontal (coronal) plane of the body at birth (Fig. B). The auricle of the left atrium in the newborn is relatively a much longer tubular flap and extends more anteriorly to overlap the pulmonary trunk than in the adult. Because of the relatively large size of the heart and the transverse orientation of its axis at birth, the attachment of the pericardium to the diaphragm is also relatively larger than it is in the adult. Although it is difficult to get X-ray films of newborn infants at the same stage of respiration, the normal cardiac diameter as seen on an X-ray film is usually about 50 percent of the side-to-side diameter of the thorax at the level of the heart (Fig. B). The upper normal limit of the cardiac diameter is usually about 5.5 cm, as seen radiologically. Actually, the transverse length of the lower border of the contracted heart is about 4.0 cm. The greatest height is about 2.0 cm and the greatest anteroposterior thickness is 3.0 cm. The heart attains its definitive structure by the end of the eighth week of fetal development. Therefore, any abnormality resulting from faulty formation and partitioning of the chambers and great vessels must occur before that time.

Foramen Ovale

The foramen ovale is an aperture that connects the posterior part of the right atrium with the left atrium throughout fetal life and for a variable period after birth. It is bounded by a ridge, the limbus, and is covered by an extensive valve. The long axis of the foramen lies in the median plane of the body, while the plane of the opening corresponds almost exactly to the frontal (coronal) plane of the body. The foramen is shown in its exact position in relation to the frontal plane of the body in Figure B; the flow of blood therefore passes through the foramen from front to back. It also passes on a slant beginning anteriorly in the right atrium, and then in an upward posterior direction, passing from front to back to end in the upper posterior part of the left atrium. The reason for the slant is that the valve of the foramen resembles a spacious coat pocket with a wide opening. Starting at the opening of the inferior vena cava into the right atrium, the valve of the inferior vena cava, the sinus venarum, and the anterior surface of the valve of the foramen ovale form the right, left, and posterior walls of a tube that has its anterior wall missing, except for a small part formed by the interatrial septum. This open-sided tube directs the flow of blood from the inferior vena cava (mostly oxygenated placental blood) into the left atrium as a fluid column or stream through the blood of the atrium that enters it from the superior vena cava and coronary sinus (unoxygenated systemic blood). Nearly all the blood from the superior vena cava goes to the right ventricle, since only 2 to 3 percent passes through the foramen ovale.

As the lungs grow during fetal development their blood supply increases. Thus there is an increasing amount of pulmonary blood flow into the left atrium. As this occurs there is a gradual reduction in the flow of blood passing from the right atrium through the foramen ovale into the left atrium. The flow of blood through the lungs is limited, due to a pulmonary vascular resistance that is related to the respiratory tubes being filled with fluid. With the first breath of air after birth the lungs expand and their blood flow undergoes a sudden increase of up to 200 percent or more. The increased pulmonary blood flow into the left atrium raises the pressure in the atrium and forces the valve against the margins of the foramen ovale and the blood within the right atrium. This completely cuts off the flow of blood from the right atrium through the foramen ovale to the left atrium. Although the physiological closure is immediate, the anatomical obliteration, where the valve fuses with the interatrial septum, is a much slower process. The foramen is obliterated in fewer than 3 percent of infants by two weeks after birth. After this the obliteration proceeds rapidly; by the fourth month it is obliterated in 87 percent of infants. About 90 percent of adults have a complete closure of the foramen.

At birth the foramen is from 4 to 6 mm in vertical length and 3 to 4 mm wide. The valve of the foramen ovale consists of flexible membranous tissue; it is actually a fold of endothelium (endocardium) enclosing a core composed of small strands of cardiac muscle fibers separated by delicate reticular and elastic fibers.

Ductus Arteriosus

The ductus arteriosus is a short arched trunk connecting the pulmonary artery with the upper part of the descending thoracic aorta. It arises as a direct continuation of the pulmonary trunk where the trunk divides into right and left pulmonary arteries. It joins the aorta on its anterolateral left side below the origin of the left subclavian artery from the aortic arch. The ductus joins the aorta at an acute angle ($30°$ to $35°$); therefore, the opening of the ductus into the aorta is greatly elongated. At the upper part of where the two join, the intervening wall extends downward to end with somewhat of a sharp, crescentric border. It is more of a fold between the ductus and aorta than a true valve. The length of the ductus is extremely variable; usually it is 8 to 12 mm long. When it is long it joins the aorta well below the arch at the level of the origin of the upper aortic posterior intercostal arteries. The diameter of the ductus fully distended with blood is about 4 to 5 mm at its origin from the pulmonary trunk. Thus it is almost equal in size to the adjacent ascending aorta, which has a diameter of about 5 to 6 mm. As the two arched arteries pass inferiorly to join, they both taper to a smaller diameter, with the aorta being slightly larger (4 mm). The ductus is usually entirely extrapericardial.

The left vagus nerve and its left recurrent laryngeal nerve branch are in direct contact with the aorta and ductus where the two arteries join. The direct relationship with the left recurrent laryngeal nerve is maintained after the ductus is transformed into a dense fibrous cord, the ligamentum arteriosum. At birth the ductus is in close relationship with the left main bronchus inferiorly, and the thymus gland anteriorly.

The microscopic structure of the ductus does not differ greatly from that of the other large arterial trunks; however, there is less collagenous connective tissue in relation to smooth muscle fibers in the tunica media, compared to the aorta. This results in the wall of the ductus being much more flexible and not so thick as that of the aorta, which allows the contraction of its circular muscle fibers to occlude its lumen.

During fetal development, when the blood flow through the developing lungs is almost nonexistent, the ductus aids the right ventricle of the heart to function at full capacity so that its musculature develops at a maximum. It does this by shunting the blood from the pulmonary trunk into the aorta. Thus the right ventricle is able to force out all the blood it is capable of ejecting into the pulmonary trunk, no matter how little blood the developing lungs are capable of receiving. There is a marked pulmonary resistance to blood flow as the lungs grow, so that near term only 5 to 10 percent of the cardiac output goes to the lungs. When the newborn infant takes its first breath of air, there is a sudden reduction in pulmonary resistance that results in an increase in pulmonary blood flow of 200 percent or more through the expanded lungs that makes the immediate closing off of the ductus not absolutely essential. Even so, the elevated blood–oxygen level associated with air-breathing by the newborn infant is related to the contraction of the ductus musculature to occlude its lumen. The hormone bradykinin appears in the blood of the newborn infant to cause the smooth muscle of the ductus to contract. The ductus does not constrict completely or all at once, because functional closure takes hours or days after birth. When the ductus is partially constricted the velocity of blood flow through it may be great enough to produce a soft, inconstant, audible murmur.

The anatomical obliteration of the lumen of the ductus arteriosus actually begins before birth with a thickening of its intimal tissue. After birth there is swelling of the tunica intima and a gradual replacement of the entire wall of the ductus with dense collagenous connective tissue. Anatomical closure of the lumen is present in 88 percent of infants two months old. By one year of age the anatomical closure is normally 100 percent.

There are about 310 ml of blood in the body of the full-term infant and about 125 to 150 ml of blood in the placenta when the cord is tied immediately after birth. When the cord is not clamped until after it stops pulsating the infant derives 50 to 100 ml of blood that it would otherwise be deprived of. The cutting off of the large placental circulation when the umbilical cord is tied and the significantly increased pulmonary blood flow (200 percent or more) occurring when the infant takes its first breath, actually results in a smaller quantity of blood within the infant to be propelled a shorter distance. Therefore, the most crucial event at birth is the expansion of the lungs with the first breath of air, rather than the alterations occurring in the vascular system. Once respiration is established, the normal vascular system is well prepared to meet the functional demands imposed upon it after birth.

Kinins are polypeptide hormones that induce the contraction or relaxation of smooth muscle. Bradykinin forms in the blood of the umbilical cord when the temperature of the cord drops at or shortly after birth. It is also formed and released by granular leukocytes in the lungs of the newborn infant upon exposure to adequate oxygen. Bradykinin is a potent constrictor of the umbilical arteries and vein and ductus arteriosus, as well as a potent inhibitor of contraction of the pulmonary vessels.

Blood

The blood volume at birth is about 100 ml per kg of body weight (300 to 400 ml). The cellular constituents of the blood of all full-term infants are quite similar. The red cells (erythrocytes) are more spherical and a little larger than those of adult blood, averaging 7 to 9 microns in diameter. The number of immature red cells in the blood of a full-term infant is relatively small. Not more than 5 percent of all nucleated cells are red cells. Immature red cells are absent in 70 percent of infants two days old and in 99.6 percent of eight-day-old infants. The red cell count at birth averages between 5 and 6 million per cc of arterial blood, with a range of 4 to 8 million. The average in adult men is 5,400,000 ($\pm$ 600,000) and 4,600,000 ($\pm$ 500,000) in adult women. The white cell (leukocyte) count per cc of blood at birth ranges from 7,000 to 40,000 with an average of 19,500, whereas it averages about 7,000 in the adult. By the eighth day after birth the range is 5,800 to 17,280 with an average of 11,500. The leukocytes and lymphocytes of the blood often are not so mature as they are later in infancy. Most of the lymphocytes are large cells with pale nuclei and abundant cytoplasm. The granular leukocytes often have less-defined nuclear lobules.

At birth the serum protein value is slightly below the adult average, with the greatest difference in the globulin fraction. The total protein value averages 5.6 gm percent in full-term infants.

While the kidney is undergoing a functional adjustment during the first week after birth, the blood urea is a little higher than normal. During the second week the blood urea reaches the normal level of 20 to 40 mgm per 100 ml of blood.

The average capillary blood value of hemoglobin at birth is about 20 gm. Most of the hemoglobin at birth is fetal hemoglobin. Adult hemoglobin is present in the blood throughout fetal life in small amounts. It begins to increase in amount shortly before birth to equal the fetal hemoglobin content of the blood at two months after birth. The amount of fetal hemoglobin is at a low level at six months after birth and at eight months it is absent.

Fetal and adult hemoglobin have about the same affinity for oxygen. However, the fetal red cell containing the fetal hemoglobin has a greater affinity for oxygen but less of an ability to release it than the adult red cell has. Thus the chief differences between the fetal and maternal red cell are in their structure and function. The greater affinity for oxygen by the fetal red cell facilitates the transfer of oxygen from the maternal to the fetal blood in the placenta.

The partial pressure of oxygen (Po_2) of the systemic arterial blood during fetal life may be as low as 20 mm Hg. It increases to about 100 mm Hg within a few minutes after the onset of breathing. At one hour after birth it is about 65 mm Hg. The partial pressure of carbon dioxide (Pco_2) in the umbilical vein blood before the onset of breathing is 42 mm Hg. The Pco_2 of the systemic arterial blood at one hour after birth is about 40 mm Hg. The pH range of arterial blood is 7.30 to 7.50.

The yolk sac is the primary site of hematopoiesis from the third week to about the sixth week of embryonic life. Granular leukocytes start to form at about the fourth week. Their production steadily rises up to birth, reaching a high level during the fifth month. Thus the blood cells up to the fourth week are only red cells. Hematopoiesis occurs in the liver at one and a half months of fetal development and in the spleen at two and a half months, with a peak level occurring at these two sites between the third and sixth months. Little if any hematopoiesis occurs in the liver at birth. It ceases in the spleen at birth, being replaced by an erythrolytic (red cell destruction) function. Hematopoiesis begins in the marrow of the developing skeleton between the second and third months, reaching a peak level at four months that is maintained until term. At birth, hematopoiesis occurs in the red marrow of all the bones of the skeleton as the primary source of nearly every type of blood cell. In the adult, hematopoiesis is limited to the red marrow of cancellous bone, chiefly the bodies of the vertebrae, the ribs, sternum, diploe of the skull, and the proximal ends of the humerus and femur. The blood does not coagulate until two and a half months of fetal development. Between two and a half and three months coagulation factors begin to be produced in the liver. Of the five factors that allow vitamin K to act effectively in coagulating the blood, three are low at birth, especially in the premature infant.

Blood Vessels

The vascular distribution in the newborn infant favors a central pooling of blood and a paucity at the periphery. The internal major arterial and venous vessels and their visceral branches of the body trunk are relatively larger than those of the limbs. The capillary networks of the skin are coarse and lack the finer control mechanisms they acquire later in life. Many of the vessels so easily visualized in the adult approach microscopic size in the newborn infant, especially those of the limbs and those supplying the periphery of the trunk.

The walls of the major arteries at birth are relatively thick, strong, and elastic, whereas those of the major veins are relatively thin, weak, and collapsible. The aortic arch and its branches—the aorta, the vena cavae, and azygous vein—are relatively larger in the newborn infant than in the adult.

A calculated increase in the diameters of the empty vessels of newborn cadavers, to arrive at what the diameters are when the vessels are fully distended with blood in the living full-term infant, follows.

Arteries	*(mm)*	*Veins*	*(mm)*
aortic arch and pulmonary trunk	5–6	internal jugular vein	3–4
ductus arteriosus	4–5	subclavian vein	3–4
pulmonary artery	3–4	brachiocephalic vein	4–5
brachiocephalic arterial trunk	4–5	superior vena cava	5–6
common carotid artery	3–4	azygous vein	2–3
subclavian artery	3–4	pulmonary vein	2–3
descending aorta	4–5	inferior vena cava	5–6
celiac artery	2–3	portal vein	3–4
superior mesenteric artery	2–3	superior mesenteric vein	2–3
renal artery (when single)	2–3	inferior mesenteric vein	1–2
inferior mesenteric artery	1–2	umbilical vein	4–5
common iliac artery	3–4	ductus venosus	4–5
umbilical artery	2–3	renal vein (when single)	3–4
internal iliac artery	2–3	common iliac vein	4–5
external iliac and femoral arteries	2–3	internal iliac vein	2–3
		external iliac and femoral veins	3–4

The bifurcation of the common carotid artery into an external and internal carotid is situated at the level of the hyoid bone in both the newborn infant and adult. Since the hyoid descends with the larynx to a lower position in the neck during early childhood, the carotid bifurcation is located at a much higher level in the neck at birth than it is in adulthood (Fig. B). The renal arteries often arise from the aorta in the newborn infant at the level between the twelfth thoracic and first lumbar vertebrae, whereas in the adult they frequently arise at the level of the upper border of the second lumbar vertebra (Fig. C). The abdominal aorta usually bifurcates into common iliacs in the newborn infant at the upper level of the fourth lumbar vertebra; in the adult it is at the lower level of the fourth (Figs. B, C). The entire length of the aorta, including the arch is about 12 cm (4¾ inches) at birth. It increases in length about three times between birth and maturity.

Umbilical Arteries

The umbilical arteries in the newborn infant are the direct continuation of the internal iliac arteries (Fig. B). As they pass along the anterior abdominal wall they elevate the peritoneum into the medial umbilical folds. At their origins from the internal iliac arteries the umbilical arteries have the same structure as other arteries of comparable size. When distended with blood their diameter at their origins is about 2–3 mm. Each is about 7.0 cm long. As the arteries approach the umbilicus their lumina become small and their walls greatly thicken. This thickening is due mainly to an increase in the number of longitudinal smooth muscle fibers of the inner part of the tunica media and an abundance of elastic fibers.

Immediately after the umbilical cord is severed, the arteries undergo a contraction so that the flow of blood from their cut ends is generally entirely arrested even though they are not ligated. The hormone bradykinin forms in the umbilical blood when the temperature of the cord drops at or shortly after birth. It is a potent constrictor of the umbilical arteries. Thrombi often form in the distal ends of the arteries. The actual obliteration of the lumina is brought about by the proliferation of connective tissue in the tunica media and intima of the vessels which begins before birth. Obliteration proceeds from the umbilicus and by the end of the second or third month after birth the vessels are usually obliterated to the level of the superior vesical arteries. The dense fibrous cords, which were once part of the umbilical arteries, are then known as the medial umbilical ligaments. The proximal parts of the umbilical arteries that are retained continue to be known as the umbilical arteries in the adult. Each gives rise to the artery of the ductus deferens and the superior vesical artery or arteries.

Umbilical Vein

The umbilical vein in the newborn infant is about 2 to 3 cm in length (Figs B, C); its diameter is 4–5 mm when distended. Passing from the umbilicus it extends upward and a little to the right to the porta hepatis where it joins the left branch of the portal vein, forming a sinus of some size. Throughout most of its course it is enclosed between the layers of the falciform ligament. Before joining the portal vein it gives off several large intrahepatic branches that are distributed directly to the liver tissue; 40 to 60 percent of the blood passing through the umbilical vein goes through the liver by way of its intrahepatic branches and its connection with the portal vein. The remainder passes through the ductus venosus.

Compared to the umbilical arteries the vein is thin-walled. A definite internal layer of elastic fibers is present in the umbilical vein at the umbilical ring, whereas in the intra-abdominal part of the vein the tunica interna is not sharply marked off from the tunica media by an elastic membrane. However, the tunica media does contain some elastic fibers among bundles of smooth muscle and collagen fibers. The umbilical vein contracts when the umbilical cord is severed but, because of the scanty amount of muscle tissue, not so vigorously as the ductus arteriosus and umbilical arteries do. The hormone bradykinin forms in the umbilical blood when the temperature of the cord drops at or shortly after birth. It induces the musculature of the umbilical vein to contract. Due to the reduced pressure in the vein compared to that of the arteries, the amount of smooth muscle, and especially the elastic tissue it contains at the umbilical ring, is sufficient to completely arrest the flow of blood from its cut end even though it is not ligated. A smooth muscle sphincter that loops around the cord vessels at the umbilical ring in a number of newborn mammals is absent in man.

During the first forty-eight hours after birth the intra-abdominal portion of the umbilical vein is partially contracted. The lumen is flattened from side to side to a very small size. However, it can be fairly easily dilated with a catheter having a 1-mm diameter. The obliterative process to transform the umbilical vein into the round (teres) ligament of the liver begins shortly before birth. A subintimal proliferation of fibrous tissue occurs around the periphery of the lumen. This new fibrous tissue, plus the contraction of the bundles of collagenous fibers of the tunica media, constitutes the bulk of the round ligament. No thrombi are involved in the obliterative process. A marked gradient in intensity of the obliterative process occurs along the length of the vein, being maximal at the umbilical end and minimal at the hepatic end. In most adults the original lumen of the umbilical vein persists throughout the round ligament that can be easily dilated to a 5- or 6-mm diameter.

Ductus Venosus

In the newborn infant the ductus venosus is a venous trunk that is a direct continuation of the umbilical vein by arising from the left branch of the portal vein, directly opposite where the umbilical vein joins it, and terminating in the inferior vena cava, or more commonly in the left hepatic vein just before it joins the vena cava. It lies within the two layers of the lesser omentum (hepatogastric ligament) in a groove or fossa between the left and caudate lobes of the liver.

In the newborn infant the ductus is located in the median sagittal plane of the body at the level between the ninth and tenth thoracic vertebrae. At birth the ductus venosus is 2 to 3 cm in length and 4 to 5 mm in diameter when fully distended with blood; 40 to 60 percent of the umbilical venous blood passes through the liver, with the remainder passing through the ductus venosus.

The ductus venosus has the structure of a muscular vein. Its thick intima is surrounded by a tunica media consisting mainly of circularly arranged smooth muscle fibers mixed with a considerable amount of elastic and some fibrous tissue. Transformation of the ductus venosus into the ligamentum venosum usually begins the second week after birth. The lumen of the ductus is completely obliterated between the second and third months after birth. The obliterative process begins at the portal vein end and extends to the vena cava. The portion joining the left hepatic vein or the inferior vena cava may be retained for an indefinite period of time after birth as a funnel-like pocket.

Esophagus

From the cricoid cartilage to the cardiac part of the stomach the esophagus in the newborn infant measures 8 to 10 cm (Fig. C). This length doubles during the first three years after birth. Then the increase is slow, with the adult length of 23 to 30 cm attained after puberty. In the newborn infant the esophagus is slightly more than one-fourth the combined length of the head and trunk, whereas in the adult it is equal to about one-sixth or one-seventh.

When measured with a catheter the average diameter of the esophagus at birth is 5 mm; its upper limit is at the level of the fourth to the sixth cervical vertebrae and the inferior limit is at the level of the ninth thoracic vertebra (Fig. C). Thus, both the upper and lower ends of the tube lie from one to two vertebrae higher in the adult. The curvatures of the esophagus are present in the newborn infant but are less pronounced than in the adult. This is also true for the normal esophageal constrictions. As in the adult, the narrowest constriction is where the esophagus joins the pharynx. At this junction the cricopharyngeal part of the striated inferior pharyngeal constrictor muscle functions strongly to constrict the lumen. Thus, this junction is commonly traumatized with probing instruments. The terminal part of the esophagus becomes the short abdominal part after it passes through the esophageal hiatus of the diaphragm to become continuous with the cardiac part of the stomach. The esophageal hiatus is formed by contributions of muscle bundles from the crura of the diaphragm. The amount each crus contributes is variable; it may be equal or shift to a predominantly greater contribution from the right crus to a point where the hiatus is formed entirely by muscle bundles from the right crus.

The esophagus of the newborn infant may have areas of ciliated columnar cells scattered about its stratified squamous epithelium, which rapidly disappear after birth.

Abdominopelvic Cavity and Peritoneum

The abdominal portion of the abdominopelvic cavity is an ovoid space in the newborn infant. The space is largest in its upper part where its transverse and anteroposterior diameters are the greatest above the level of the umbilicus (Figs. B, C). Both of these diameters are relatively greater in comparison to the length of the abdominal cavity and to the total length of the body than they are in the adult. The circumference of this body region is about 35 cm (12 inches). The posterior extensions of the cavity on either side of the vertebral column are much less pronounced than they are in the adult. The adult vertebral column projects quite far inward so that the anteroposterior distance between the vertebral bodies and the sternum is relatively much less compared to the transverse diameter of the cavity than it is in the newborn infant. The reduction in the anteroposterior diameter of the lower part of the cavity, caused by the lumbar curve of the vertebral column, is practically absent at birth. Therefore, from an anterior view the posterior wall of the abdominal cavity appears to be quite shallow. The anterior surfaces of the kidneys in the newborn infant, which are situated in the relatively shallow parts of the abdominal cavity on each side of the vertebral column, face more anteriorly than in the adult, where they face more laterally.

The thoracic skeleton of the newborn infant contributes relatively much less protection to the abdominal cavity than it does in the adult. The xiphoid process in the adult overlaps the anterior part of the cavity by as much as one or two vertebral levels more than in the newborn infant. Also, the distal ends of the eleventh ribs are almost in direct contact with the iliac crests laterally in the adult, whereas they are widely separated in the newborn infant (Fig. A).

The pelvic portion of the body cavity at birth is very small both absolutely and relatively compared to that of the adult (Figs. A, B, C). It is more elongated than in the adult and almost circular in cross section. The pelvic cavity forms less of an acute angle with the abdominal cavity at birth because of the absence of a lumbar curve and the presence of only a slight sacral curve (Fig. C). Due to the small size of the pelvic cavity at birth the pelvic viscera are in a higher position than in the adult. Structures that are within the pelvic cavity in the adult occupy a position almost entirely within the infant's abdominal cavity, especially the urinary bladder, ovaries, and uterus (Figs. B, C); the rectum is the only part of the intestinal tract that lies in the pelvic cavity. Nearly all of the anal canal and vagina project inferiorly beyond the inferior pelvic aperture (Fig. C).

The peritoneal attachments and reflections at birth are, in general, not much different in adulthood. The apron of the greater omentum in the newborn infant is relatively very small (Fig. C). Its lower margin rarely extends much below the level of the umbilicus at birth and contains little if any fat; thus it is a delicate, semitransparent, double-layered membrane in which the fusion of the two layers is usually incomplete.

The attachment of the root of the mesentery for the jejunum and ileum in the newborn infant becomes less curved and more vertical with the elongation of the lumbar region occurring during childhood. The length of the mesentery from the posterior abdominal wall to the jejunum and ileum is relatively greater at birth than in adulthood, and the length of the transverse and sigmoid mesocolons, from the wall to the viscus, is relatively great. In contrast, the area of attachments of the ascending and descending colons to the posterior wall is relatively much smaller than in the adult. The mesentery of the small intestine and the mesocolons of the large intestine contain little if any fat at birth.

The peritoneal reflections of the newborn urinary bladder vary greatly with the filling and emptying of the bladder. When the bladder is empty and contracted, the reflection over it from the anterior abdominal wall is about midway between the umbilicus and pubic symphysis (Figs. B, C). However, when the bladder is fully expanded with urine the peritoneal reflection may lie as high as the umbilicus. The peritoneal fold of the bladder, the transverse vesical, is usually quite evident in the infant with an empty bladder. The depth of the peritoneal reflections, forming the rectovesical pouch in the newborn male and the vesico-uterine pouch in the newborn female, is usually relatively greater than in the adult (Fig. C). The rectovesical pouch may extend so far inferiorly that a part of the posterior surface of the prostate gland has a peritoneal investment.

As soon as the future abdominal cavity forms in the embryo it fills with watery fluid. Thus the peritoneal cavity of the young fetus is distended with a watery peritoneal fluid. As the end of gestation approaches, the amount of fluid decreases, but there may be a relatively large amount that is absorbed during or a short time after birth. The peritoneal cavity then becomes essentially a potential space with its approximated serous membranes separated by a thin layer of friction-reducing viscous peritoneal fluid.

At birth the retroperitoneal subserous connective tissue is condensed in the region of the kidneys, suprarenal glands, ureters, and gonadal vessels in the form of the layers of the renal fascia that enclose these structures. The anterior layer of renal fascia is made up of delicate areolar tissue that is intimately fused with the peritoneum. The posterior layer is a distinct sheet of more dense connective tissue. At birth there is little if any perirenal fat between the two layers of renal fascia encapsulating each kidney. In the vicinity of each kidney in the newborn infant there is a relatively large mass of brown fat—the adipose capsule or pararenal fat pad which is situated between the posterior layer of renal fascia and the transversalis fascia that serves as the internal parietal lining of the entire abdominopelvic cavity. The pararenal fat pads support the kidneys in their proper position within the abdominal cavity in both the newborn infant and adult. The importance of the brown fat to the newborn infant is discussed with the adipose tissue. In this book the pararenal fat is treated as a part of the adipose capsule of the kidney because the official terminology (Paris, *Nomina Anatomica*) does not recognize the renal fascia as a specific structural modification of the sub- or retroperitoneal fascia. If the renal fascia is treated as a structural entity it is more appropriate to regard the perirenal fat, which is virtually absent in the newborn infant but completely encapsulates the adult kidney, as the adipose capsule, excluding the pararenal fat body. If the renal fascia is not recognized, the perirenal and pararenal fat are appropriately grouped into a more or less common mass surrounding the kidney, the adipose capsule.

Stomach

The only time the shape, size, and position of the stomach can be described with any degree of accuracy in the living newborn infant is immediately after birth (Figs. B, C). As soon as the infant cries it swallows large amounts of air into the stomach. Once the infant swallows both liquid and air the stomach may easily increase in size to four or five times that of the empty, contracted state. The distended stomach also shifts its position within the abdomen in relation to the position of the body and the state of expansion or contraction of the other abdominal viscera.

All the subdivisions of the adult stomach are present in the stomach of the fetus before birth. The mucosal folds, including the longitudinal ones along the lesser curvature, disappear when the stomach is fully expanded.

The anatomical capacity of the stomach is between 30 and 35 ml at birth and about 75 ml the second week; at the end of the first month it is about 100 ml or three times that of the infant at birth. The average stomach capacity of the adult is 1,000 ml.

The mucosa and submucosa of the stomach of the newborn infant are relatively much thicker than they are in the adult (Fig. C). The total number of gastric glands at birth is about 2 million; it is over 25 million in the adult. Acid secretion begins before birth and the proteolytic activity of the gastric glands in the newborn infant is less than 20 percent of the value found in the infant two to three months old.

The musculature of the stomach, including the pyloric canal and sphincter, are only moderately developed at birth. The longitudinal muscle layer is thin and may be incomplete over a part of the greater curvature. Elastic tissue is very poorly developed. Contractions of the stomach musculature occur as the stomach develops in the fetus. However, the peristaltic activity is abnormal. The progressive peristaltic contraction wave is absent in the newborn stomach; instead, there is a simultaneous nonperistaltic contraction of most of the stomach musculature.

Intestinal Tract

The shape and arrangement of the intestinal tract in the abdominal cavity are quite different in the newborn infant than in the adult. When the opened abdomen of the newborn is viewed anteriorly the intestines appear as an oval-shaped mass bounded above by the liver and left costal margin and below by the brim of the pelvis. Because of the great relative width of the abdomen and the large size of the liver, the greatest diameter of the anterior surface of the intestinal mass is transverse in the newborn infant, whereas it is vertical in the adult. When the anterior abdominal wall is intact, the intestinal mass is indented below in the midline by the abdominal portion of the urinary bladder (Fig. C). The only part of the large intestine in the newborn infant that can be seen anteriorly is a portion of the transverse colon that is partially hidden by the inferior border of the left lobe of the relatively massive liver, and a part of the sigmoid colon that abuts the lowest part of the anterior abdominal wall on the left side. The empty stomach is usually completely hidden anteriorly by loops of jejunum shortly after birth.

The weight of the intestinal tract emptied of its contents is about 10 gm in a seven-month fetus. During the last two months of fetal life the weight of the tract increases at a rapid rate so that the average in the full-term infant is nearly 50 gm. In the adult the average weight of the intestinal tract is about 490 gm, or nearly ten times greater than that of the newborn infant.

The average length of the intestinal tract at birth, from the pylorus to the anal canal, is 338.5 cm (11 ft), with a range of from 336 to 461 cm (14½ ft). The tract increases about a third in length during the first year after birth. Thereafter, the growth rate is much less. The length of the intestines in the adult is about twice that of the newborn infant. The ratio of the length of the intestinal tract to the length of the entire body is much greater in the newborn infant (8.3 : 1) than in the adult (4.5 : 1 or 5.5 : 1). The change in its relative length is due not so much to the reduced rate of its lineal growth as to the rapid growth of the lower limbs, because if the length of the tract is equated with that of the trunk there is little difference between the newborn infant and the adult. The ratio between the length of the small and large intestines remains almost unchanged between birth and adulthood.

The surface area of the intestinal tract increases about four times between birth and adulthood. In the newborn infant the villi are distributed throughout the entire small intestine just as they are in the adult. The villi increase rapidly in number during the latter part of fetal life to about one million at birth. Villi continue to form up to puberty when the adult number of 4 to 6 million is reached. When the villi are established, between the fourth and fifth months of fetal development, epithelial cells proliferate from the lining cells of the glands between the villi. The new epithelial cells migrate along the villi from their bases to their tips where they are shed into the lumen. Once started, this process of renewing the epithelium of the villi continues throughout the life of the individual.

Lymphatic tissue is present at birth throughout the intestinal tract, including the vermiform appendix. It is usually in the form of diffuse masses without definite germinal centers. There is a marked increase in the amount of lymphatic tissue during the first year, and germinal centers appear within a few weeks after birth.

The elastic tissue of the intestinal tract of the newborn infant is confined almost entirely to the walls of the blood vessels. It increases greatly in amount in the intestinal wall during the first few months after birth.

The most remarkable feature of the intestinal tract at birth is its thin wall. This is due chiefly to the comparatively weak development of its musculature. There is a disproportion in the relatively greater thickness of the mucosa and submucosa as compared to the muscle layer. The ratio of mucosa and submucosa to muscle in the newborn infant is 23:26, whereas in the adult it is 27:41. The longitudinal muscle layer is particularly thin in the newborn intestinal tract. The duodenal musculature is no thicker than that of the jejunum at birth. Although quite thin, the musculature of the colon is relatively better developed.

Even though the intestinal tract has poorly developed supporting musculature, it does have well-developed secretory and absorbing surfaces. A major uptake of the amniotic fluid continuously excreted by the kidneys is by absorption through the fetal intestinal epithelium. The fetus near term swallows as much as 750 ml of amniotic fluid every 24 hours; an abnormality that interferes either with the swallowing of amniotic fluid or its absorption by the fetal intestinal mucosa is associated with the accumulation of excessive amounts of amniotic fluid in the amniotic (chorionic) sac (hydramnios, polyhydramnios). Along with amniotic fluid a lot of other material is brought into the intestinal tract where it accumulates in the colon, such as sloughed epithelial cells from the skin, sloughed cells from the oral cavity and from the upper intestinal tract and respiratory tubes, lanugo hairs, fatty material from the sebaceous gland secretion of the skin (vernix caseosa), secretions of the gastrointestinal glands and of the liver and pancreas, occult blood, mucoproteins, mucopolysaccharides (including blood group substances), steroids, urea, and a sufficient amount of biliverdin to give a green color to the foregoing conglomerate known as meconium. Meconium first accumulates in the intestinal tract of the four- to five-month fetus. Because of the absorption of fluid by the intestinal mucosa, especially in the colon, the meconium becomes increasingly firm, solid, and dark in color toward the end of gestation. At birth there may be 60 to 200 gm of viscid, sticky meconium, dark greenish-brown to black, that fills almost the entire colon. A redundant sigmoid colon distended with meconium at birth often has a diameter of 2 to 3 cm.

Although there is enough peristalsis of the fetal intestinal tract to allow for some development of its musculature and to move the constituents of the meconium to the colon, it is sluggish, weak, and discontinuous. The meconium usually is suspended at the transverse folds of the rectum. Normally the fetus does not defecate until after birth. Usually the infant first defecates within ten hours after birth. Ninety-four percent of full-term infants have their first defecation within 24 hours after birth. Anoxia of the fetus before birth is a general stimulator of its intestinal motor activity. Peristalsis of the fetal colon induced by anoxia could cause the meconium to move into the anal canal and set up the defecation reflex, resulting in the relaxation of the anal sphincter muscles and the passage of meconium into the surrounding amniotic fluid. Meconium in the amniotic fluid is often a sign of fetal distress except when it appears late in labor with a breech presentation.

Although the stomach and intestinal tract are in many respects underdeveloped at birth, the digestive system of a normal full-term infant has the functional capacity to propel, digest, and absorb every type of food in liquid form, except complex carbohydrates.

Small Intestine

The small intestine, subdivided into the duodenum, jejunum, and ileum, has a total length of from 300 to 350 cm (10 to 12 ft) at birth. Its length increases about 50 percent during the first year after birth and is doubled at puberty. In the adult it averages a little over 6 meters (20 ft).

The duodenum is from 7.5 to 10.0 cm in length at birth. Its width when empty is about 1.0 to 1.5 cm (Figs. B, C). The inferior margin of the loop of the duodenum often is about 1.0 cm above the right iliac crest of the pelvis. The size of the major and minor duodenal papillae is larger in relation to the duodenum than it is in the adult. The minor papilla is frequently absent. The relatively thin-walled duodenum lacks circular folds throughout its length, and the superior part when dilated forms a relatively smaller bulb or cap in the infant.

The jejunum constitutes the proximal two-fifths of the rest of the small intestine in the newborn infant. As in the adult, there is a gradual transition to what is known as the ileum that constitutes the distal three-fifths of the small intestine (Fig. C). The width of the empty jejunum is about 1.5 cm, whereas the width of the empty ileum is about 1.0 cm or slightly less. The upper part of the jejunum is usually wider than the empty colon, except for the cecum. Although there are numerous differences in the adult between the jejunum and ileum, in the newborn infant they differ at the gross level only in size. Both are thin-walled, have virtually no circular folds, and usually have little or no fat in their attached mesentery. They do have their own vascular pattern in their attached mesentery, as the adult has.

Large Intestine

The large intestine is subdivided into the cecum and vermiform appendix, the ascending, transverse, descending, and sigmoid colons, rectum, anal canal, and anus. As in the adult, the term large intestine does not refer to the empty contracted colon of the newborn, because the empty upper jejunum of the small intestine is wider. However, the large intestine is larger than the small intestine at birth when it is distended with meconium. The length of the large intestine at birth is about 66.0 cm (2 ft), whereas it is 1.5 to 1.8 meters (5½ ft) in the adult. At birth the empty large intestine averages about 1.0 cm in width except for the cecum, which averages about 1.7 cm.

The cecum at birth is relatively as well as absolutely smaller than in adulthood (Fig. B). Its average capacity at birth is 2.5 ml and its average length

is 1.5 mm. There is no sharp demarcation between the cecum and the vermiform appendix in most newborn infants. The cecum tapers into the appendix
by an ill-defined conical termination of the cecum. The tenia of the cecum
are present at birth but the haustra and appendices epiploicae are absent.
The haustra appear during the first six months after birth; however, it is not
until the third or fourth year that the typical sacculated cecum of the adult
appears.

The vermiform appendix at birth has a diameter of from 2.0 to 6.0 mm
and a length of from 2.0 to 8.0 cm. Therefore the appendix at birth is relatively and may be absolutely larger than that of the adult. The average length
of the adult appendix is 9.0 cm, with a range of from 2.0 to 20.0 cm (Fig.
B). The position of the appendix in the abdominal cavity varies at birth as
much as it does in adulthood. The outer layer of longitudinal muscle uni-
formly surrounding the appendix leaves the appendix to pass along the large
intestine to the rectum chiefly as three longitudinal bands, the tenia coli.
The three separate tenia are relatively underdeveloped at birth. There is always a thin sheet of longitudinal muscle between the tenia in the newborn
infant and adult.

The ascending colon is relatively as well as absolutely shorter in the newborn infant than in the adult (Fig. B). This is not due to the position of the
cecum but to the small dimensions of the lumbar region at birth. The ascending colon in the newborn infant is 1.0 cm wide when empty.

The transverse colon is relatively long at birth; when empty it is about
14.0 to 15.0 cm in length (Figs. B, C). At birth it is 1.0 cm wide when
empty.

The descending colon is relatively short and yet it is twice the length of
the ascending colon (Fig. B). This is associated with a much higher position
of the left colic flexure compared to the right flexure. The descending colon
at birth is 1.0 cm wide when empty.

As in the adult, the sigmoid colon is quite long. In the newborn infant it
may be as long as the transverse colon, or about 14.0 to 15.0 cm when empty
(Fig. B). Part of the sigmoid colon usually makes contact with the lower-
most part of the anterior abdominal wall on the left side. In about 50 percent of infants a part of the sigmoid lies in the right iliac fossa. Although the
empty sigmoid colon is 1.0 cm wide at birth, it is usually greatly distended
with meconium before the first defecation (2.0 to 3.0 cm wide). Since the
pelvic cavity is too small to contain any part of the sigmoid colon when it is
distended, it projects far up into the abdominal cavity.

The ascending, transverse, descending, and sigmoid colons have certain
features in common at birth that differ in adulthood. At birth the tenia coli
are not well developed, the walls are thin due to poor muscular development,
and their external surfaces are smooth even when they are empty and con-

tracted because they lack sacculations (haustra) as well as attached appendices epiploicae. The haustra appear during the first six months after birth.

The rectum is relatively longer in the newborn infant than in the adult. The upper part of the rectum is usually directed to the right, whereas the lower part descends vertically and is straighter than in the adult (Fig. C). The empty rectum in the newborn infant is 1.0 cm wide. At birth the upper part of the rectum is usually distended with meconium in the region of the rectal folds.

The junction of the rectum and anal canal forms almost a right angle at birth. The anal canal lies completely outside the inferior aperture of the pelvis, below the tip of the coccyx (Fig. C). The anal canal is relatively longer at birth than in adulthood. The anus is located a little posterior to its position in the adult (Fig. C). The anal columns, sinuses, and valves are all differentiated before birth (Fig. C). The outer longitudinal smooth muscle layer of the colon, which has three thickened muscular bands in it, the tenia coli, becomes a uniform layer without tenia in the wall of the rectum and anal canal, just as it does in the wall of the vermiform appendix. The muscular part of the wall in the rectum is relatively very thin at birth. It is much thicker in the wall of the anal canal where the inner circular smooth muscle layer of the large intestine becomes thicker to form the internal anal sphincter. The internal sphincter is surrounded by a layer of striated muscle, the external anal sphincter (Fig. C).

Although the anal sphincter musculature is relatively well developed before birth, it may not have to function forcefully or continually when the meconium is confined by the rectal folds to the rectum. Abnormally, when anoxia of the fetus occurs, it induces active peristalsis of the colon and rectum to propel the meconium into the anal canal. This initiates the defecation reflex and the anal sphincter musculature relaxes to allow the passage of meconium into the amniotic fluid.

Liver

The liver of the full-term infant usually weighs between 90 and 140 gm, with an average weight of 120 gm. The weight of the liver is more than doubled during the first year and tripled during the third year after birth. By the time of puberty the weight has increased ten times. The total increase in the weight of the liver is twelve to thirteen times between birth and adulthood. The liver constitutes about 4.0 percent of the body weight at birth, 3.0 to 4.0 percent during most of childhood, and 2.5 to 3.5 percent in adulthood.

As in the adult, the liver is the largest gland in the body. At birth it occupies about two-fifths of the abdominal cavity. The greatest vertical length of the right lobe is about 6.0 cm and the thickness is about 6.0 cm. The distance between the right and left sides of the entire liver is about 7.5 cm. It fills the entire upper part of the cavity, occupying more of it on the right side than on the left (Figs. B, C). The liver is in direct contact with the greater part of the diaphragm at birth, extending as high as the fifth rib in quiet respiration at the midclavicular line on the right side (Figs. B, C). Its inferior border extends anteriorly below the costal margin for a considerable distance (Figs. B, C). Its inferior border often extends posteriorly as low as 1.0 cm above the iliac crest of the pelvis. Since the respiratory changes in the size of the thorax of the newborn infant are due mainly to the movement of the diaphragm, the liver, by being attached to the diaphragm through the falciform, triangular, and coronary ligaments, must move with the diaphragm (Fig. C). Other factors that participate in maintaining the liver in direct contact with the diaphragm at all times are the attachment of the inferior vena cava to the diaphragm, the attachment of the hepatic veins to the inferior vena cava and, especially, the force of the muscular part of the anterior abdominal wall acting indirectly on the liver through all of the abdominal viscera.

As in the adult, one component of the liver consists of flexible and compressible parenchyma; the other component comprises sinusoids and vessels filled with blood. The shape of the liver in a living individual at a given time is therefore directly influenced by adjacent structures, such as the stomach, small intestine, ascending and transverse colons, and spleen, which are continually undergoing changes in size and shape.

The left lobe constitutes a little over one-third of the liver in the newborn infant. In later childhood it constitutes from one-third to one-fourth and in the adult one-fifth. However, as in the adult, according to the internal morphology of the liver the quadrate lobe and part of the caudate lobe belong to the left lobe. Although the liver appears to be structurally mature at birth, it is functionally immature. For example, because of certain enzyme deficiencies in the liver of the newborn infant, especially if premature, it cannot handle the bilirubin load presented to it when there is exaggerated breakdown of the red cells of the blood after birth. This results in the transient physiological jaundice (icterus) of the newborn. Also, the liver at birth is not making sufficient quantities of the necessary factors that allow vitamin K to act effectively in coagulating the blood.

The formation and development of blood cells (hematopoiesis) occurs in the fetal liver after one and a half months of development, with a peak between the third and sixth months. Few if any blood cells are produced in the liver of a full-term infant.

Gall Bladder

The gall bladder of the newborn infant is relatively small; its length is about 2.0 cm and its maximum width 1.0 cm. It is usually more embedded in the liver substance than the adult's, and it has a proportionately smaller peritoneal surface (Fig. B). The gall bladder at birth may be crossed by bands of liver substance that often undergo involution later in life. Often the fundus does not extend to the margin of the liver in the newborn infant. The capacity of the gall bladder increases rapidly during the first two years after birth when it acquires the same relative size in comparison to the liver weight as in the adult. From then on the increase in the liver weight and gall bladder capacity is proportional.

Pancreas

In the newborn infant the pancreas weighs from 3 to 5 gm. During the first two months after birth the gland increases little in mass, but between the third and sixth months its weight is doubled. By the end of the first year it weighs about 10 gm. The weight of the pancreas in the adult is over thirty times that of the newborn infant.

The pancreas is from 4 to 6 cm in length and from 1 to 2 cm in thickness at birth. The adult subdivisions of head, neck, body, and tail are present; however, there is no sharp demarcation between the body and tail. The head forms a somewhat greater part of the gland in the newborn infant than in the adult (Figs. B, C). The surface markings are less pronounced at birth than in adulthood. The inferior margin of the head is level with the second lumbar vertebra and the body and tail usually angulate upward as they pass to the left. Because the vertebral column of the newborn infant does not project into the abdomen as much as it does in the adult, there is less of a curve in the body of the pancreas as it passes from an anterior to a posterior direction. As in the adult, the tail of the pancreas usually is in contact with the hilus of the spleen.

The exocrine acinar cells and the endocrine islet cells appear about the third month of fetal life. By three and a half months of fetal development the islet cells produce insulin. The exocrine function of the gland, especially in the premature infant, usually has not achieved adult values at birth. The relative number of pancreatic islets (Langerhans) is greater in the newborn infant than in the adult. There are a little more than 120,000 pancreatic islets in the newborn pancreas, whereas there is an average of over 800,000 in the adult.

Spleen

The average weight of the spleen at birth is 13 gm, with a range of from 5 to 15 gm. The spleen doubles its weight during the first year after birth. The weight is tripled at the end of the third year. The total weight increase from birth to adulthood is about twelve times.

In the newborn infant the long axis of the spleen is generally vertical or oblique (Fig. B). The size of the spleen is as variable as its weight at birth; the average in the full-term infant is 4.5 cm in length, 2.0 to 2.5 cm in width, and 1.0 cm in thickness. Accessory spleens are very common in the newborn infant; they are usually located in the greater omentum, especially in its gastrosplenic ligament portion.

The formation and development of blood cells (hematopoiesis) occurs in the spleen between two and a half months of fetal life and birth, with a peak level between the third and sixth months of development. As the production of blood cells ceases at term it is replaced by an erythrolytic (red cell destruction) function. The development of the white pulp of the spleen is directly related to the presence of a functioning thymus gland in the fetus.

Kidneys

The weight of both kidneys at birth is between 20 and 35 gm. This weight is doubled by the sixth month, quadrupled by the second year, and increased by eight times at puberty. The average weight of the kidneys in the adult is from ten to fourteen times that of the newborn infant. Although the absolute weight increase is great, the kidneys decrease in relative weight from birth to adulthood. The right kidney is usually heavier than the left at birth.

At birth the kidneys average 4.0 to 5.0 cm in length, 2.0 to 2.5 cm in width, and 1.2 to 1.5 cm in thickness. They increase in length and width about two and a half times and in thickness about two times between birth and adulthood. The kidneys are a little thicker proportionately in the newborn infant than in the adult.

Both the skeletal and visceral relations of the kidneys are quite different in the newborn infant than in the adult (Fig. B). The differences in the skeletal relations are due mainly to the large size of the kidneys and the shortness of the lumbar portion of the posterior abdominal wall. In two-thirds of newborn infants the left kidney is in a slightly higher position than the right one (Fig. B). The superior margins of the kidneys are usually level with the intervertebral disc above or below the twelfth thoracic vertebra at birth. The inferior margins of the kidneys in 50 percent of newborn infants are below the level of the iliac crests of the pelvis, in 25 percent they are level with the crests, and in 25 percent they are above the crests. By the second year after birth the lower margins of the kidneys are all above the iliac crests.

The kidneys in the newborn infant have lobulated surfaces. The number of lobules varies anywhere from five to twenty-five. They usually disappear by the fourth or fifth year of age, although some may persist in the adult. The lobules represent the renal lobes of which the kidney is originally composed; however, at birth there is no relation between the number of lobules and the number of renal papillae.

Since the vertebral column does not project as far into the abdomen in the newborn infant as in the adult, much more of the anterior surfaces of the kidneys faces anteriorly than in the adult, where the anterior surfaces face more laterally. In the adult the renal arteries and veins, situated anterior to the kidneys, have to pass in a more direct anteroposterior direction to get to the kidneys than they do in the newborn infant. The branches of the renal vascular segments are established long before birth.

In the newborn infant the cortex is one-fifth to one-fourth the thickness of the medulla, in the adult it is one-half to two-thirds. The last of the more than one million glomeruli and associated convoluted tubules appear in each kidney at the time of birth. Therefore, the growth of the kidney after birth is the enlargement of existing functional units rather than an increase in their number.

The kidneys have no essential function during fetal life because the excretory requirements of the fetus can be completely satisfied by the placenta. Fetuses structurally normal except for the complete absence of kidneys go on to full-term development. However, there is a virtual absence of amniotic fluid when the fetus lacks kidneys. Normally, the kidneys of the fetus three and a half months old form urine. From this time on to term the fetal kidneys make an increasingly greater contribution to the amniotic fluid in the form of urine.

At birth the glomeruli appear to be the adult type; however, not all of them are functioning at birth. The filtration rate of the kidney is less than normal until about six weeks after birth when all the glomeruli become fully functional and the overall filtration rate reaches that of the adult. The ability of the kidneys of the full-term infant, and especially the premature, to excrete water, sodium, and hydrogen ions is less than that of the adult. However, the kidney function is efficient in the young infant with a normally watery diet. While the kidney undergoes a functional adjustment during the first week after birth, the blood urea level is a little higher than normal. During the second week the blood urea reaches the normal level of 20 to 40 mgm per 100 ml of blood.

Ureters

The ureters are from 6.5 to 7.0 cm long in the newborn infant, or a little less than one-fourth as long as they are in the adult (Fig. B). The ureters practically double in length during the first two years after birth as the lumbar region of the body grows. The widest diameter of the ureter at birth is always relatively and sometimes absolutely greater than that of the adult. The diameter is about 2.0 mm at the isthmus and 5.0 mm in the lumbar part of the abdominal portion. There is usually an abrupt reduction in the diameter to about 2.0 mm where the abdominal portion becomes the pelvic portion (Fig. B).

Longitudinal folds of the mucosa develop in the empty and contracted pelvis of the kidney and its continuation, forming the upper part of the ureter.

Suprarenal Glands

The relative size of the suprarenal glands is great at birth (Fig. B); they form about 0.2 percent of the entire body weight in the average full-term infant as compared with 0.01 percent in the adult. The average actual weight of the two glands is about 9.0 gm, whereas the average in the adult is 7.0 to 12.0 gm. As in the adult, the left gland is generally heavier than the right.

At birth the suprarenal glands are usually from 2.0 to 2.5 cm in length, 2.5 to 3.5 cm in width, and 0.8 to 1.0 cm in thickness. In the adult the length is usually 2.5 to 3.5 cm, the width from 4 to 5 cm, and the thickness 1.0 cm or a little less. The two glands have about the same differences in shape as they have in the adult, and the left is larger than the right.

The topography of the suprarenal glands at birth is quite different from that of adulthood. This is due mainly to their large size at birth. As in the adult, part of the right gland is located against the diaphragm in the bare area for the liver.

The medulla of the gland is relatively small at birth. In contrast, the cortex is relatively much thicker than it is in the three-month fetus and the adult. At birth two parts of the cortex can be distinguished—there is a bulky fetal cortex and a thin overlying true or permanent cortex. The fetal cortex disappears during the first year after birth with an accompanying loss in size and weight of the glands. By the end of the second week after birth the average weight of both glands drops from the birth weight of 9.0 gm to about 5.0 gm. In the period between two weeks and three months after birth the weight of both glands averages 4.36 gm. The initial birth weight is not regained until puberty.

Corticosteroids are produced by the cortex of the suprarenal glands between the eighth and ninth weeks of fetal development. Before birth the medulla of the glands produces insignificant quantities of epinephrine. This is in contrast to the medulla after birth, which becomes almost the exclusive source of epinephrine.

The large size of the fetal suprarenal cortex is related to the active interplay it has with the placenta. Before birth the fetal cortex cannot produce progesterone. Maternal cholesterol is converted in the placenta successively into pregnenolone and then to progesterone. The fetal cortex utilizes progesterone as a substrate and processes it into a variety of other substances, including both androgens and corticosteroids. The newborn infant is relatively deficient in these substances because the infant's progesterone-producing system has not developed to the point where it can completely replace the placental supply of that substrate. The fetal cortex is a main source of the androgens dehydroepiandrosterone (DHA) and its hydroxylated form, 16-α-OH-DHA, which are precursors of the estrogen, estriol. Estriol is produced in relatively large amounts by the placenta.

Bony Pelvis

The structural features that constitute the bony pelvic sexual dimorphism of adult bony pelvises are absent at birth. The general form of the newborn pelvis is that of a cone. The length is somewhat greater in proportion to the greatest transverse and anteroposterior diameters than it is in the adult and the pelvic cavity is relatively much smaller. The dimensions of both the lesser (true) pelvic cavity and the inferior pelvic aperture are smaller in proportion to the superior pelvic aperture in the newborn infant than in the adult. The anteroposterior diameter of the inlet of the true pelvis is about 2.8 cm and the transverse diameter is 2.2 cm. The distance between the inlet and outlet is 2.0 cm. The anteroposterior diameter of the outlet is about 1.5 cm and the transverse diameter 2.0 cm.

The sacrum forms a greater proportion of the pelvic circumference than in the adult (Fig. A). It is less depressed between the ilia, and the sacral promontory is less apparent and located at a higher level, than in the adult.

The alae of the ilia are relatively thick and rounded in the newborn infant and extend upward abruptly. The iliac fossae are present at birth but very shallow.

The obturator foramina are relatively small and are closer together than in the adult. The whole pelvis is more vertical in position at birth. The plane of the superior aperture (inlet) forms an angle of 80° with the horizontal plane as compared with 60° in the adult. Related to this the pubic symphysis is also much more vertically oriented than in the adult (Fig. C). The acetabula are relatively very large at birth but much shallower than in adulthood; the vertical diameter is between 12.0 and 15.0 mm and the transverse diameter between 11.0 and 12.0 mm. The depth at its center is between 6.0 and 7.0 mm. The head of the femur is always larger than the acetabulum so that almost a third of the head is external to the acetabulum.

During the first two years after birth the pelvis grows rapidly in all dimensions. Until the infant assumes the erect position and begins to walk, the form of the pelvis changes little. When this occurs the sacrum begins to descend between the ilia, and the promontory becomes established. The sex differences of the bony pelvis, which result in the larger birth canal of the female, begin to appear at puberty. The sex differences are due mainly to the deviation of the shape of the pelvis in the male away from the genetic agonadal type, which is the female type. The chief factor in the male that induces the formation of the male-type pelvis is androgen. Males who are physiological castrates from birth to adulthood have female-type bony pelvises.

The coxal bone is really a complex, composed of three bones: the ilium, ischium, and pubis. At birth the superior ramus of the pubis, the ramus of the ischium, and a greater part of the body of the ilium are ossified (Fig. A). The three ossifying bones are separated by a broad Y-shaped cartilage forming the bulk of the acetabulum. The three main bones and one or more acetabular ossification centers merge with one another between the fourteenth and sixteenth years after birth.

The sacrum is about 3.3 cm long and 2.3 cm wide at its upper part at birth. The sacrum consists of five segments, each of which corresponds to a vertebra. These cartilaginous segments are separate at the time of birth and each contains five ossification centers corresponding to one for the body, two neural arch components, and two costal components of the free vertebra (Fig. A). The costal and neural arch ossification centers merge with those of the body between the second and sixth years after birth and the neural arch centers of each side fuse medially between the seventh and fifteenth years.

The coccyx is about 6.0 mm long at birth. An ossification center appears in the body of the first segment of the coccyx shortly before or after birth (Fig. A). The center for the fourth, and usually the last segment of the coccyx, appears at puberty.

Urinary Bladder

At birth the contracted urinary bladder is a fusiform organ that is broad below and gradually tapered above to where it is continuous with the obliterated urachus (allantois) of development, the median umbilical ligament (Figs. B, C). The apex of the contracted bladder in the newborn infant is at a point midway between the pubis and umbilicus. The long axis of the bladder in the newborn infant is nearly vertical and measures about 3.0 cm. It is 2.0 cm wide at its base. There is no true fundus in the bladder at birth as there is in adulthood. A distinct interureteric fold is present in the contracted bladder of the newborn infant.

At birth the bladder contains only a small amount of urine. The fully distended bladder in the young infant is almost completely an abdominal organ and may extend upward to the level of the umbilicus.

Internal Male Reproductive Organs

The prostate gland is relatively much larger in the newborn infant than in the adult (Fig. B), due mainly to the fact that the pelvic cavity is relatively so small at birth. Other than the rectum the prostate is the only major organ occupying the pelvic cavity in the newborn male. It is similar to the uterine cervix of the newborn female in shape, size, and the position it occupies in the pelvic cavity (Figs. B, C). The prostate at birth weighs about 0.82 gm; it is about 1.4 cm wide in the transverse plane, 1.0 cm in vertical length, and 7.0 mm thick anteroposteriorly. Its dimensions are tripled between birth and adulthood. The prostatic urethra at birth is about 1.0 cm in length. It is three times longer in the adult.

The seminal vesicles are relatively large in the newborn male, as are the adjacent ampullae of the ductus deferens (Fig. B). Both seminal vesicles weigh about 0.05 mg at birth. Each seminal vesicle is about 2.0 mm thick and 7.0 mm long.

Internal Female Reproductive Organs

During the later part of fetal life the ovaries grow very rapidly. Their combined average weight in the newborn female is about 0.3 gm. They double their weight during the first six weeks after birth. The total increase in weight between birth and adulthood is about sixteen times.

The ovaries are relatively very large at birth (Fig. B)—from 1.5 to 3.0 cm in length and 4.0 to 8.0 mm both in width and thickness. Thus newborn ovaries are much larger than newborn testes. In the adult the ovaries are flattened and almond-shaped, between 2.5 and 3.5 cm long, 2.0 cm wide, and 1.0 cm thick. The ovaries in the newborn female are generally triangular in cross section in the central portions and rounded at the ends. They have surface furrows that disappear during the second and third months after birth. The ovaries at birth are relatively higher in position than in adulthood, occupying a position in the lower part of the iliac fossae. Each passes downward over an external iliac artery into the ovarian fossa below the artery during early childhood. The long axis of the ovaries in the newborn female is almost vertical. During their descent after birth the long axis becomes horizontal and when they reach their permanent position in the ovarian fossae the long axis becomes vertical again.

Any estrogen secretion by the ovaries before birth is insignificant. Maternal estrogen crosses the placenta, and fetal estrogen is of little consequence in the differentiation of the female genitals compared to the influence androgen has in the male. Germ cells (future ova) appear in the gonads (future ovaries) during the fifth week of fetal life. At about the middle of fetal life primordial follicles begin to appear in the gonads and at term most of the germ cells have been converted into primordial follicles. In fact, some of the follicles at birth have developed to the point that they have a thick layer of granulosa cells and central cavities of varying sizes. They may even be grossly visible as follicles with a diameter of several millimeters. Occasionally the central cavity of a single follicle contains more than the usual amount of fluid and measures 1.0 cm or more in diameter. There is a peak total of 3 to 6 million ova in the ovaries of the female fetus. Atresia of ova begins before birth so that there are only about 300,000 ova in the newborn female. This number is maintained until puberty. Atresia of ova occurs during follicle formation throughout the reproductive period of the female when only 300 to 400 follicles ever reach full maturity and rupture.

At birth the uterus is from 2.5 to 5.0 cm in length, with an average of 3.5 cm. It is about 2.0 cm at its widest point between the uterine tubes, about 1.3 cm thick, and weighs between 3 and 4 gm (Figs. B, C). The body of the uterus is proportionately small. The cervix forms about two-thirds or more of the length of the uterus, the isthmus between the body and cervix is absent, and the fundus is relatively small. The uterine cavity is a narrow slit-like cleft that is flattened anteroposteriorly and the thickness of the uterine mucosa (endometrium) varies from 0.5 to 1.5 mm. The endocervical glands of the cervical canal undergo secretory activity before birth to the extent that the cervical canal is usually distended by a plug of tenacious mucus. The dilatation of the cervical canal by the mucous plug may cause the canal to become as much as 1.0 cm wide.

During the first few weeks after birth the uterus, which had been affected by the maternal hormones before birth, undergoes a marked involution in which the length decreases about one-third and the weight decreases over one-half. This involution is due mainly to an atrophy of the uterine muscle. The size and weight of the uterus at birth is not regained until the beginning of puberty. After puberty the adult dimensions are attained when the length is about 7.5 cm, the width 5.0 cm, and the thickness 2.5 cm.

In the newborn female the uterus is wedged into the narrow pelvic cavity between the base of the urinary bladder and the rectum (Fig. C). Therefore its position depends upon the state of these organs. At birth the urinary bladder contains only a small amount of urine, but the rectum is distended with meconium. As a result, the uterus is pressed forward (anteverted).

The uterine tubes at birth are relatively short and wide (Fig. B). Each is about 5.0 mm wide at the ampullae and 3.0 cm long. In the adult each tube is 10.0 cm long.

The vagina at birth is from 2.5 to 3.5 cm in length and about 1.5 cm wide in the region of the fornices (Figs. B, C). The uterine cervix extends about 1.0 cm into the vagina. The vagina is distinctly curved in the newborn infant; the posterior wall is therefore longer than the anterior wall which makes the vagina appear shorter when viewed from the front or back than from the side. The cavity of the vagina at birth is only potential because the longitudinal columns are enlarged and covered with a thick layer of cornified, stratified, squamous epithelium (Fig. C). In contrast, the stratified squamous epithelium of the hymen, which forms the elliptical orifice of the vagina, is thin, smooth, and uncornified (Fig. C). Even though the vaginal walls are approximated, they can be greatly expanded to a circumference of 4 to 5 cm. In contrast, the distensibility of the orifice of the vagina is much less. The orifice and hymen are described with the external female genitals.

After birth, when the stimulus of the maternal pregnancy hormones is terminated, the cornified cells of the vaginal epithelium are sloughed. The lumen between the orifice and the fornices is reduced to a transverse slit. The orifice remains a sagittal cleft and the lumen at the fornices is circular. Although changes occur in the vagina after birth, they are not so marked as those occurring in the uterus. The vagina grows very slowly in childhood. Just before puberty rapid growth begins and continues until adult dimensions are attained. In the adult the anterior wall is about 7.5 cm in length and the posterior wall is 9.0 cm.

Lower Limbs

The lower limbs are relatively underdeveloped at birth, both structurally and functionally. They are proportionately smaller compared to the adult and tend to be positioned by the newborn infant as they were before birth, with the limbs flexed and abducted at the hip joints, the knees flexed, and the feet inverted in the talipes varus position. In fact, the newborn infant strongly resists the straightening of its lower limbs. Although the legs appear bowed, this is an illusion created by the position of the limb joints and the shape of the soft tissues, because the tibia and fibula are straight (Fig. A). The distance between the hip joint and the heel of the extended limb is about

16.5 cm (6½ inches). The part of the limb between the knee and heel (leg) is relatively very short at birth. The distance between the knee and ankle is about 7.5 cm (3 inches).

The position of the lower limbs before birth promotes the not uncommon disorder of congenital dislocation of the hip, which can also occur during and after parturition. The dislocation occurs more frequently on the right side and in Caucasian females. At birth the neck of the femur is very short and forms a much more acute angle with the body or shaft than in adulthood. In newborn infants only part of the relatively large head of the femur is lodged in the acetabulum, and the ligament of the head of the femur is relatively very long. With the ligament intact, the head of the femur can easily be completely removed from the acetabular cavity laterally but not displaced posteriorly. Therefore the chief factors resisting the posterior dislocation of the hip joint are the thin articular capsule of the hip joint and its relatively weak intrinsic supporting ligaments, and the ligament of the head of the femur. With the thighs in continuous abduction before birth the adductor muscles that act to resist hip dislocation are more or less on the stretch. This accounts for part of their underdevelopment at birth. Related to this is the relative underdevelopment of all the muscles of the lower limb that are to function powerfully in walking, especially the gluteal muscles of the buttocks and the gastrocnemius and soleus muscles of the calf.

The body or shaft of the femur at birth is quite straight, whereas in the adult it is always bent in a gentle arch with its concavity directed backward. This bend is acquired with the assumption of the erect posture. The length of the femur at birth is about 8.5 cm (3½ inches). The widest circumference of the head is between 3.9 and 4.5 cm.

Unlike the carpal bones of the wrist, which are not ossified at birth, two bones of the ankle, the calcaneus and talus, always have an ossification center at birth (Fig. A). There is a 50 percent chance that an ossification center is present in the cuboid at birth.

As with the upper limb, there is an orderly sequence of the appearance of ossification centers, which occur earlier in females than males. Some centers appear relatively late; for example, the centers for the patella occur between three and six years and those for the sesamoid cartilages of the big toe appear during the eighth year in females and the eleventh year in males.

As early as the second month of fetal life the foot is strongly inverted; at about the seventh month a process of gradual eversion begins, although at birth and for some time thereafter some inversion is still present. Eversion of the foot is brought about by profound changes in the shape of the calcaneus and talus, and by the rapid growth of the bones forming the medial border of the foot. However, it is common for one or both feet to be inverted (pigeon-toed) to a noticeable degree in adulthood. At birth the foot has a greater degree of dorsiflexion than in later life. This is due to the relatively greater area of the trochlea of the talus. In contrast, plantar flexion of the foot is relatively limited, due, in part, to the shortness of the extensor muscles of the foot of the newborn infant.

The feet are relatively long and narrow. The length from the heel to the tip of the big toe is about 6.5 cm (2½ inches). The maximum width is 2.5 cm (1 inch). The sole is markedly tapered at the heel.

The footprint of the newborn infant outlines almost the entire plantar area, like the footprint of a flat-footed adult. This is due to the thick plantar fibrous fat pad that conceals definite longitudinal and transverse arches. In fact, the longitudinal arch is relatively higher in the newborn infant than in the adult. There is an absolute and relative decrease in the height of the longitudinal plantar arch during the second year after birth when the child first begins to bear weight upon its feet.

As early as the fourth month of fetal development epidermal ridges are present in the skin of the plantar surface of the sole and toes that will serve to increase the friction of the skin surface after birth. In each fetus the lines of epidermal ridges form distinct patterns (toe prints) unlike those of any other human being.

Figure A. Ossified Portions of the Full-term Newborn Skeleton

1. Anterior fonticulus (fontanelle)
2. Frontal bone
3. Coronal suture
4. Sphenoid fonticulus
5. Roof of orbit
6. Fossa for lacrimal sac
7. Nasolacrimal canal
8. Floor of middle cranial fossa
9. Pterygoid process
10. Infraorbital foramen
11. Hard palate
12. Enamel of deciduous teeth
13. Mandibular canal
14. Mental foramen
15. Body of hyoid bone
16. Tympanic part of temporal bone
17. Clavicle
18. Scapula
19. Humerus
    a. head
    b. body
    c. olecranon fossa
20. Ulna
21. Radius
22. Bodies of metacarpal bones
23. Bodies of phalanges
24. Coxal bone
    a. ilium
    b. ischium
    c. pubis
25. Center in talus
26. Center in calcaneus
27. Parietal bone
28. Lesser wing of sphenoid bone
29. Posterior fonticulus
30. Optic canal
31. Squamosal suture
32. Hypophyseal fossa of sphenoid bone
33. Squamous part of temporal bone
34. Lambdoidal suture
35. Mastoid fonticulus
36. Subarcuate fossa
37. Internal acoustic meatus
38. Spheno-occipital synchondrosis
39. Petrous part of temporal bone
40. Occipital bone
    a. squamous part
    b. lateral part
41. 6th cervical vertebra (3 centers)
42. 1st rib
43. Centers of sternum (superimposed upon thoracic vertebrae)
44. 12th rib
45. 3rd lumbar vertebra (3 centers)
46. Centers in sacrum
47. Center in coccyx
48. Femur
    a. body
    b. condylar center
49. Tibia
    a. condylar center
    b. body
50. Fibula
51. Bodies of metatarsal bones
52. Bodies of phalanges

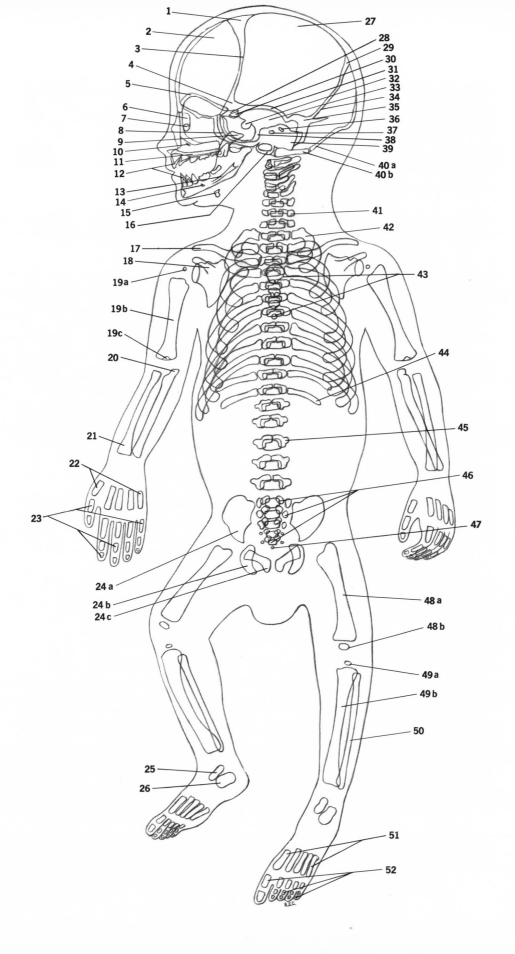

Figure B. Topographic Anatomy of a Full-term Newborn Infant

1. Superior sagittal dural sinus
2. Right cerebral hemisphere
   a. frontal lobe
   b. temporal lobe
3. Eyeball
4. Ethmoid air cell
5. Maxillary sinus
6. Nasal cavity
7. Infraorbital foramen
8. Enamel of deciduous teeth
9. Bifurcation of common carotid artery
10. Internal jugular vein
11. Clavicle
12. Thymus gland
13. Right lung
14. Mammary gland areola
15. Foramen ovale
16. Right atrioventricular valve
17. Right border of heart
18. Superior border of liver and central level of diaphragm
19. Posterior inferior level of lung
20. Xiphoid process
21. Right suprarenal gland
22. Right kidney
23. Gall bladder
24. Transverse colon
25. Duodenum
26. Anterior inferior border of liver
27. Ascending colon
28. Umbilical vein
29. Ileum
30. Appendix
31. Cecum
32. Right ovary
33. Uterine tube
34. External iliac artery
35. Right umbilical artery
36. Right half of uterus
37. Urethra
38. Vagina
39. Hymen
40. Left lateral ventricle
    a. central part
    b. anterior horn
41. Interventricular canal
42. 3rd ventricle
43. Left lateral ventricle
    a. posterior horn
    b. inferior horn
44. Zygomatic arch
45. External acoustic meatus
46. Tympanic membrane
47. Mental foramen
48. Thyroid cartilage
49. Cricoid cartilage
50. Thyroid gland
51. Left lung
52. Trachea
53. 2nd costal cartilage
54. Auricle of left atrium
55. Pulmonary valve
56. Aortic valve
57. Left border of heart
58. Left atrioventricular valve
59. Esophagus
60. Stomach (empty)
61. Spleen
62. Pancreas
63. Duodenojejunal flexure
64. Left ureter
65. Descending colon
66. Aorta
67. Sigmoid colon
68. Umbilical cord
69. Median umbilical ligament
70. Umbilical artery
71. Common iliac artery
72. Urinary bladder
73. Ductus deferens at deep inguinal ring
74. Left seminal vesicle
75. Left half of prostate gland
76. Epididymis
77. Left testis
78. Scrotum

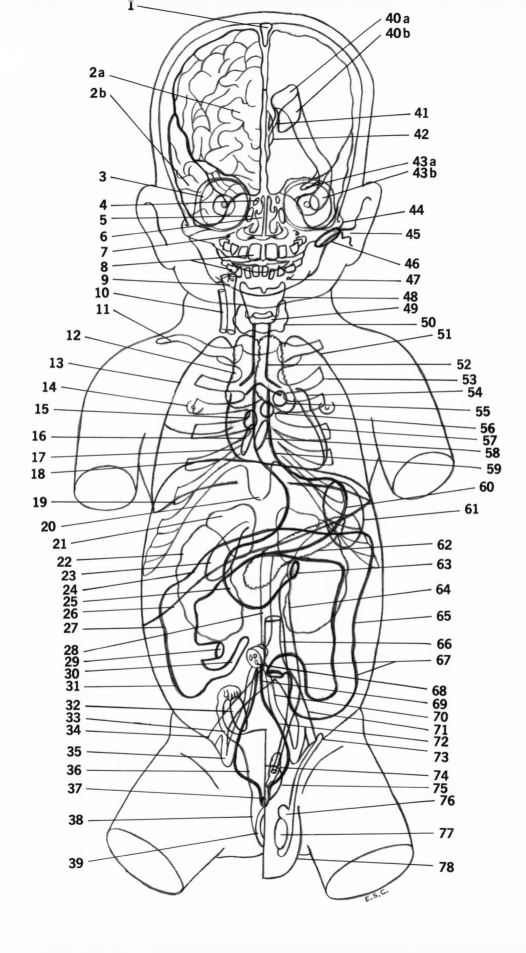

Figure C. Midsagittal Section of a Full-term Newborn Female

1. Superior sagittal sinus
2. Falx cerebri
3. Corpus callosum
4. Septum pellucidum
5. Right interventricular foramen
6. Frontal lobe of right cerebral hemisphere
7. Optic nerve
8. Hypophysis
9. Olfactory nerve
10. Cribriform lamina
11. Sphenoid bone
12. Nasal cavity
13. Ostium of auditory tube
14. Naris
15. Hard palate
16. Foramen cecum of tongue
17. Mandible
18. Hyoid bone
19. Laryngeal ventricle
20. Vocal fold
21. Thyroid cartilage
22. Cricoid cartilage arch
23. Isthmus of thyroid gland
24. Left brachiocephalic vein
25. Thymus gland
26. Sternum
27. Auricle of right atrium
28. Aortic semilunar valves
29. Right ventricle
30. Pericardium
31. Liver
    a. left lobe
    b. caudate lobe
32. Pylorus of stomach
33. Gastrocolic ligament
34. Transverse colon
35. Transverse mesocolon
36. Greater omentum (apron)
37. Jejunum

38. Falciform ligament
39. Umbilical vein
40. Stump of umbilical cord
41. Median umbilical ligament
42. Ileum
43. Urinary bladder
44. Pubic symphysis
45. Vesico-uterine pouch
46. Clitoris
47. Urethra
48. Vagina

---

49. Superior cerebral veins
50. Thalamus protruding into 3rd ventricle
51. Pineal body
52. Great cerebral vein
53. Cerebral peduncle
54. Cerebral aqueduct
55. Straight sinus
56. Pons
57. Spheno-occipital synchondrosis
58. 4th ventricle
59. Confluence of sinuses
60. Cerebellum
61. Medulla oblongata
62. Ligamentum nuchae
63. Median aperture of 4th ventricle
64. Nasal part of pharynx
65. Lamina and spinous process of 2nd cervical vertebra
66. Oral part of pharynx
67. Soft palate
68. Epiglottis
69. Laryngeal part of pharynx
70. Arytenoid cartilage
71. Cricoid cartilage lamina
72. Subcutaneous adipose tissue (interscapular brown fat)

73. Trachea
74. Brachiocephalic trunk
75. Ascending aorta
76. Openings of right pulmonary veins in left atrium
77. Coronary sinus
78. Left ventricle
79. Esophagus
80. Diaphragm
81. Coronary ligament
82. Spinal medulla (cord)
83. Cardiac part of stomach
84. Lesser omentum
85. Omental bursa
86. Splenic artery
87. Opening of right renal artery in aorta
88. Left renal vein
89. Pancreas
90. Splenic vein
91. Duodenum
92. Nucleus pulposus of intervertebral disc between 2nd and 3rd lumbar vertebrae
93. Filum terminale among spinal nerve roots (cauda equina) within vertebral canal
94. Body of 5th lumbar vertebra
95. Uterus
96. Rectum
97. Sacrum
98. Median sacral artery
99. Sacral hiatus
100. Recto-uterine pouch
101. Coccyx
102. Rectovaginal septum
103. Anal canal
104. Anococcygeal ligament

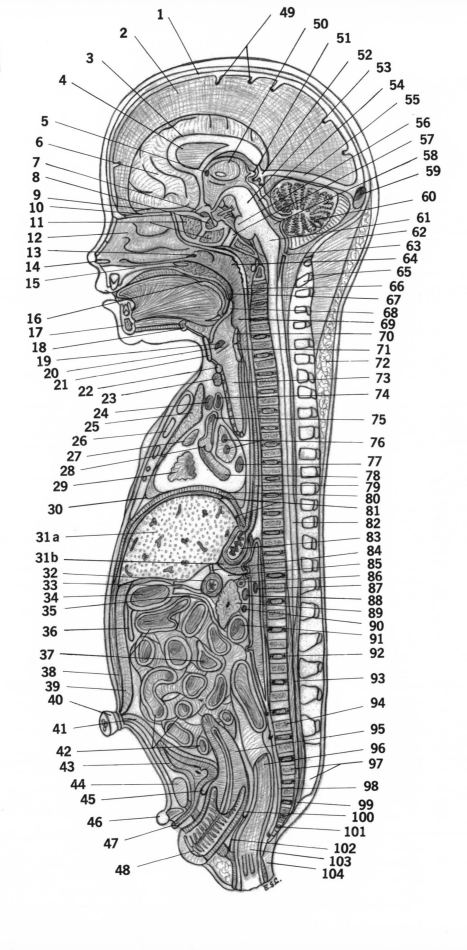

1
2
3
4
5
6
7
8
9
10
11
12
13
14
15
16
17
18
19
20
21
22
23
24
25
26
27
28
29
30
31 a
31 b
32
33
34
35
36
37
38
39
40
41
42
43
44
45
46
47
48

49
50
51
52
53
54
55
56
57
58
59
60
61
62
63
64
65
66
67
68
69
70
71
72
73
74
75
76
77
78
79
80
81
82
83
84
85
86
87
88
89
90
91
92
93
94
95
96
97
98
99
100
101
102
103
104

E.S.

Index